Miami's Dark Tales

Miami's Dark Tales

By
Kalila Smith

Miami's Dark Tales

Copyright © 2013 Kalila Smith

Cover design by Lori Osif and Allan Gilbreath

All rights reserved. No part of this book may be reproduced, duplicated, copied, or transmitted in any form or by any means without the express written consent and permission of the editor and publisher.

This is a work of fiction. The names, characters, places, and incidents are fictitious or are used fictitiously. Any resemblance to any person or persons living or dead is purely coincidental.

Published by
Dark Oak Press
Kerlak Enterprises, Inc.
Memphis, TN
www.darkoakpress.com

ISBN 13: 978-1-937035-57-0
Trade Paperback
Library of Congress Control Number: 2013948463
First Printing: 2013

Special thanks to everyone at Dark Oak Press for all of the encouragement and assistance.

This book is printed on acid free paper.

Printed in the United States of America

Acknowledgements

Thanks to everyone in Miami and Key West who contributed to the investigations, interviews, and experiences that made this book possible.

Table of Contents

Preface 1
Introduction 5
Gangster Paradise 13
The Devil's Triangle 19
Crimes of Passion 25
Serial Killers 35
The Devil Made Them Do It 43
For God's Sake 57
Local Haunts 65
Haunted Hotels 73
Haunted Houses 79
Tropical Poltergeist 89
Ghosts of the Glades 95
Strange Creatures 103
Real Monsters of the Everglades 109
Visitors from Afar 117
Close Encounters 125
The Mystery of Coral Castle 131
The Lady in Blue 137
Haunted Highway 145
Island of Bones 149
Spirits of Key West 155
Memories of Papa 163
Haunted La Concha Hotel 169
Ghosts of the Gulf 173
Geiger's Ghosts 177
Dolly Dearest 183
Strange Love 191
Resurrection 201
Final Thoughts 211
Bibliography 215

"Everyone moves to Miami to die." ~ Dexter

Preface

The rising sun burned my face as I awoke sweaty and mosquito-bitten after a not-so-comfortable night of sleeping in my van. The one bad thing about hurricane evacuations is that there is never a guarantee where you might wind up in order to secure a hotel room. I pressed the button bringing my seat back up into an upright position and gazed across the crowded convenience store parking lot. I felt relieved that I wasn't the only one who couldn't find a hotel the night before. I had spent countless hours driving around Louisiana in search of a hotel room the previous day. The closest one would have required an eight hour drive to Dallas; a trip I didn't care to make. My decision forced me to settle for sleeping in the van, with the dogs I had in tow, and the mosquitoes. I called a co-worker from the tour company back in New Orleans to assess the situation. After hearing that the hurricane had merely grazed the city and all was well, I headed back home feeling thankful that I had opted not to drive all the way to Houston.

I drove back to my home in St. John Parish in the aftermath of Hurricane Katrina to find a fence down, a roof leak, and no electricity. But even with no power, it beat being stuck in a hotel in Dallas with my menagerie.

The following morning I received a phone call from my employer informing me that there was water gushing up from the uptown manholes. A couple of hours later, he called again to let me know that he was moving the computers and files upstairs. The water was rising inside the building and at that moment, the tour company no longer existed. I hung up, stunned. What did that mean? Did he just fire me? I turned on the television to see every New Orleanian's worst nightmare. The 17th Street Canal wall had breached and Lake Pontchartrain was pouring into the city. This was the big one we had dreaded our entire lives.

For months, I waited to see what was to be the fate of New Orleans. I suggested to the owner that we launch another tour company in another city to offset what had happened in New Orleans. At that time my intent was to investigate and get the new location off the ground then return to New Orleans and continue to get it back up and running.

After much research of various tourist hot spots, Miami seemed to be the best candidate. I had always loved Miami, especially South Beach. Like New Orleans it had a vibe all its own. It was also a port city, like New Orleans, drawing tourists in from all over the world.

Miami was the backdrop for many popular television shows such as Dexter, CSI: Miami, Miami Ink, and home to numerous celebrities making it the Hollywood of the East Coast. I set forth on my adventure to research and document the weird, the ghostly, and the macabre in the Miami area and found a plethora of mysteries along with a rich history.

Although the company ultimately decided not to open a branch tour office in the area, a book on the mysterious city was well overdue. What follows is by no means an exhaustive study of Miami's darker side; it is merely a survey of the major points of interest for the seekers of seediness, ghouls, and gore.

Introduction

Miami has had its share of Indian wars, yellow fever epidemics, hurricanes, and murders. Tequesta and Seminole tribes had inhabited the area for at least 10,000 years. The city's name is derived from Lake Mayaimi, now Lake Okeechobee, which means "big water."

During the 15th century, Spain was the leader in the age of discovery. Conquistadors traveled the world in search of new opportunities for commerce and conquest. In 1492, Christopher Columbus discovered an island directly off the coast of Eastern Florida. Columbus made several voyages to the New World over the next several years. It was on his second voyage in 1493, that a young explorer, Juan Ponce de Leon, joined him.

Born in San Servas, Spain, in 1460, Ponce de Leon fought in southern Spain against the Moors at the end of the 15th century. He left Spain for adventures in the New World shortly after the fall of Grenada. He followed Columbus on his second voyage which led him to the island of Hispaniola. Lured by rumors of gold on the island of Borinquen, now Puerto Rico, he traveled on, brutally conquering the island and becoming governor. In 1511, he was removed as governor and within two years, left Boriquen in search of a legendary spring of eternal youth believed to be somewhere on the island of Bimini. It was on this excursion that he became the first European to see the Miami area, which he called Chequescha, as he sailed into the Biscayne Bay.

On April 2, 1513, he landed in what is now St. Augustine. He called the land Pascua de Florida (feast of flowers) in honor of Palm Sunday, the day he first spotted the lush vegetation of the area. The natives were very resistant to Spanish invasion. The local tribes drove Ponce de Leon out of Florida at which point he returned to Puerto Rico and resumed fighting with indigenous tribes of the island until being mortally wounded in battle.

Pedro Menedez De Aviles visited Miami's Tequesta settlement in 1566 in search of his missing son who had shipwrecked somewhere in the area. He built a mission there the following year. A fort was built nearby in 1743.

The untamed wilds of South Florida made a perfect hideaway for the treasures of infamous pirates such as Jean Lafitte, Blackbeard, Captain Kidd, Sir Henry Morgan, and others. South Florida beaches are believed to harbor more buried and sunken treasure than any other U.S. state. Most of the treasures are from pirates but others, especially during wars, buried their fortunes to protect them from the enemy. When they died, they took their secret locations with them.

Over the years, fishermen, divers, and diggers have stumbled across millions of dollars of gold and silver either buried or on sunken Spanish Galleons.

There are countless stories of Spanish coins washing up on shore after hurricanes and tropical storms.

Pirates were sea thieves who attacked ships and maritime cities throughout the Gulf of Mexico and the Caribbean. Spain held the most wealth in these areas so it was Spain that was usually robbed. Pirates stole not only treasures but would overtake entire ships, killing the captains and crews. They would hide their contraband throughout the New World in coastal regions.

A large portion of pirate income was made through slavery. Often pirates would kidnap their victims and sell them to other countries as slaves. Sometimes investors or governments would hire pirates as privateers, (pirates with a letter of mark from an imperial government or colonial administration) to attack an enemy. Privateers were usually involved with commercial ventures but a pirate by any other name is still a criminal.

In 1715, English Buccaneer Samuel Bellamy came to South Florida in search of treasure. Failing to find what he wanted, he turned to piracy as Captain Black Bellamy. He robbed over fifty ships in the bay including one called *The Whydah* which was carrying thousands of dollars of gold, silver, and ivory. Bellamy claimed *The Whydah* as his flagship shortly before a storm hit. A forty foot wave capsized the vessel swallowing up Bellamy and his new-found fortune.

William Rogers, A.K.A. Bowlegs Billy, was infamous in South Florida. Originally one of Jean Lafitte's privateers, he fought alongside Andrew

Jackson at the Battle of New Orleans in 1815. He later fought in Florida in the Seminole War. Afterwards, he and his Choctaw wife returned to Oklahoma for several years. He later returned to Florida where he worked as a fisherman during the week and a pirate on weekends.

His ship, *The Mysterio*, sunk by British troops, went down with over four million dollars in silver bars onboard.

One of the most notorious of all Miami pirates was Black Caesar. He was believed to be an African Chief who had been tricked onto a slave ship. He escaped during a hurricane and set up a base camp somewhere in the keys. He was rumored to keep a harem of over one hundred women. Best known for robbing ships near Cuba and the keys, he buried most of his treasure deep in the Everglades. In 1798, he buried a shipload of silver bars on Key Largo. He forced the crew members to dig the hole to bury the treasure then killed all of them, burying them with the silver.

Early settlers told of ghostly galleons appearing off the shore then disappearing. Many a settler ventured deep into the Everglades in search of hidden treasures, never to be seen again. A local legend tells of a ghostly mist that appears in the swamp leading to buried treasure and curses unleashed by those who find them.

There can certainly be non-paranormal explanations for the disappearance of those lurking into the swamp; alligators, crocodiles, poisonous snakes, quicksand, to name a few. It is most likely greed and stupidity to blame for these mysterious disappearances rather than ghosts and pirates' curses. Locals claim to see ghostly schooners off the shorelines of Miami and South Florida. Pirates were just the beginning of the area's turbulent history.

In 1868, a Pennsylvania farmer, Henry Lum, purchased 165 acres of beach property for $.75 an acre for a coconut farm. Twenty years later, his son, Charles, built the first home in South Beach at 12th Street and Ocean Drive. Dense mangroves and hordes of mosquitoes made farming in the area nearly impossible. The Lums abandoned South Beach leaving their plantation in control of a wealthy Quaker farmer, John Stiles Collins.

Miami is the only major American city to have been planned by a woman. A native of Cleveland, Ohio, Julia Tuttle purchased a large plantation in Miami in 1891. She pressured railroad tycoon Henry Flagler to expand his railroad from St. Augustine to Miami. Flagler showed no interest. She spent two years enticing him to expand the railroad, always being met with rejection.

In 1894 a great freeze hit Florida destroying citrus crops all across the state except in Miami. Julia Tuttle seized the opportunity to literally turn lemons into lemonade. She wrote to Flagler sending him a sprig of orange blossoms noting that Miami was untouched by the freeze. This time Flagler took notice and expanded his railroad to Miami. On July 28, 1896, the city of Miami was incorporated.

In January, 1897, Henry Flagler opened his new Royal Palms hotel and began promoting Miami as the

American Riviera. Miami began to grow as a winter getaway for the wealthy and famous. Some disasters, however, cannot be escaped.

Yellow fever epidemics spread rapidly throughout the Southeastern United States all throughout the 1700 and 1800s. Similar to the Black plague of Europe the disease remained a mystery until the twentieth century. A massive epidemic hit Miami in 1899 killing thousands. Many of those who had not contracted the disease left the area. But disease was only the beginning of disaster in Miami. Hurricanes were also a major cause of death in South Florida.

On September 18, 1926, at approximately 2:00 AM, a hurricane devoured Miami Beach with one hundred fifty mile an hour winds. The U.S. Weather service called it "the most destructive hurricane to ever strike the United States." Spanning over sixty miles, the massive storm destroyed not only Miami but nearby Fort Lauderdale, Hollywood, and Hallandale. The wind howled as the tide rose and flooded the first floors of hotels and buildings along the beach. One visitor recalled her windows broken out by the wind. She watched in horror as the sheets were literally ripped off her bed. Entire buildings collapsed as flood waters rose over roads. By 6:30 AM, the eye of the storm was over the city. Unaware of the lull of the eye, many people left the safety of buildings in attempts to evacuate. Some even drove over bridges and causeways.

Thirty-five minutes later, the backlash of the storm swept over the island with more ferocity than before. Tidal waves washed out roads and bridges swallowing up vehicles and their passengers. The death toll was estimated between three hundred twenty-five and eight hundred. The majority of people living in the projected path were new to Florida. Having never experienced a hurricane, they had little knowledge of its destructive force or the price they would pay for their ignorance.

By 1929, South Beach was the gambling capital of the South. Even during prohibition, alcohol flowed freely in bars and casinos. The freewheeling lifestyle of Miami Beach attracted notorious gangsters, like Lucky Luciana, the Giancana and Genovese families, Frank Costello, and Al Capone; many of whom made South Beach their second home. For the next several years, Miami became the crime capital of the South.

Gangster Paradise

"I am like any other man. All I do is supply a demand." ~ Al Capone

Al Capone was called everything from "Public Enemy Number One" to "the greatest gang leader in history." Having orchestrated dozens of murders, he was a legend in his own lifetime. He operated speakeasies and prostitution rings in Chicago, New York, and Miami. He spent his winters in a sprawling mansion on Palm Island.

In Chicago, Capone maintained an appearance of respectability living a modest life in a middle class neighborhood. He passed himself off as a salesman. But in Miami, he was feared. Residents and authorities alike worried that his presence would have a negative effect on tourism for the resort town. Capone turned Miami Beach into a hotbed for rum running, gambling, and prostitution. The city of Miami called his home "a menace to the safety and well-being of residents." The state of Florida declared martial law and ordered the immediate arrest of Capone.

Capone was arrested and released several times in Miami. While being under scrutiny for one murder, he managed to arrange his most notorious crime, the St. Valentine's Day Massacre. On the morning of February 14, 1929, as Capone was held in questioning in Miami, seven men gathered in the garage of George "Bugs" Moran in Chicago.

The group had met there to collect a shipment of bootleg liquor that was on its way from Detroit. As they waited for Moran, they had no idea of what horror lie ahead for them. The meeting was actually a setup. Rather than a shipment of booze, several police pulled up in front of the home and began walking up towards the garage.

After ordering the seven to line up against a wall, the cops pulled shotguns and machine guns from their coats and began blasting away. Witnesses would remember blood splattered everywhere, smearing the wall and pooling on the cold cement floor. "Only Capone kills like that," Moran said when told of the slaughter. Capone was sunning on the beach in Florida at the time of the murders, but he'd set up the hit that became legendary in American criminal history. Al Capone was said to have believed that the ghosts of the massacre haunted him the remainder of his life.

In May 1929, Capone was arrested in Philadelphia for carrying concealed weapons and sentenced to a year in the Eastern State Penitentiary. He served only eight months but long enough for IRS Special Intelligence Unit to use his Miami home as proof of his income. Eliot Ness, leader of the "Untouchables," simultaneously gathered evidence of his bootlegging activity.

Capone returned to Miami in 1930 continuing to bootleg all the while trying to improve his public image by hosting goodwill dinners. In 1931, Capone was found guilty of 22 counts of tax evasion and sentenced to 11 years in prison.

In 1934, he was moved from a federal facility in Atlanta to Alcatraz Prison. He had served only six and half years of his sentence when he was released on parole.

He returned to Miami suffering from dementia and other symptoms of advanced syphilis. He died in his Miami home on January 25, 1947, one week after his 48th birthday.

Although both Alcatraz and Eastern State Penitentiary claim to be home to Capone's ghost, no doubt the ghost of the notorious mob boss prefers his Miami home for his ghostly stomping ground. Through the years, various residents of the home claimed to have heard pots and pans banging in the kitchen late at night, lights going on and off and a voice believed to be Capone's. Some have felt the sensation of someone climbing into bed with them.

The Clay Hotel on Washington Avenue is the former location of Capone's Miami Casino. It's the same hotel where eighteen-year-old Desi Arnaz started the rumba craze in Miami. Desk clerks believe that Capone and his cronies walk the halls late at night. Strange sounds emit from the top floor, now an internet Café. Footsteps are often heard late at night, but the room is usually empty upon examination. There have been numerous reports of a woman dressed in 1920s attire wandering about the top floor and in the stairwell. During my stay, scraping sounds and loud bangs could be heard. It was as if furniture was being moved in the wee hours of the morning. Interestingly, none of my neighbors at the hotel heard anything.

One ghost in the hotel is believed to be that of another mobster, Johnny Roselli, a former thug for Capone. Roselli was called "the man who knew too much." But it wasn't knowing too much that got Johnny killed, it was talking too much about what he knew. His death is the most mysterious in Miami's history. Conspiracy theorists still try to pinpoint who murdered him.

Johnny began his career with Capone then became a trusted employee of Sam Giancana. He worked for years as a liaison between the two. In the late 1930s, he was arrested for extorting one million dollars from Hollywood movie companies then again in the 1960s for running crooked card games in L.A. But it was what Johnny called doing his "patriotic duties" that got him the most attention, probably the wrong kind at that. The CIA called it "Operation Mongoose."

In 1960, the CIA contacted Roselli and Giancana via Howard Hughes' assistant about a special assignment to assassinate Fidel Castro. Most of the work fell on Roselli. Roselli met with them at the famed Fontainebleau Hotel on Collins Blvd. The hotel was a favorite hangout for mobsters in earlier years and during the 1960s a hotspot for celebrities such as Frank Sinatra, Sammy Davis Jr., Peter Lawford, Dean Martin, and Joey Bishop, otherwise known as the Rat Pack. The CIA gave him money, guns, and poison pills for Castro. In return, Roselli gave them a lot of talk.

Miami's Dark Tales

A Castro aid was supposed to have slipped him the poison but backed down, a waiter was supposed to have put it in his food but Castro stopped going to that restaurant. Another hit man was set to give the Cuban leader a poisoned milk shake but like the first, backed down. A group of snipers in Havana setup on a building wound up being spotted and arrested. Johnny claimed to have attempted the assassination personally by taking a high speed boat to Cuba but that the boat was shot from under him. He was rescued and taken back to Miami by another boat. In the 1970s, there was a security leak about the operation and that's when Johnny began talking.

In 1975, he testified three times before Congress. He interviewed with syndicated columnist, Jack Anderson about assassination plots. He rumored to U.S. Senators that mobster Santo Trafficante had joined Cuban Communists in the assassination of JFK. It was Trafficante, again at the Fontainebleau Hotel, that the CIA had used in another failed Castro assassination attempt. He too was given poison for Castro. After taking their money however, Trafficante flushed the pills down the toilet and disappeared. Several days before Sam Giancana was to testify before a U.S. Senate Committee, he was found shot to death in his basement. Johnny continued to talk.

Johnny Roselli was seventy-one-years-old in July of 1976 when his sister last saw him as he left for a golf game saying he'd return for dinner. He was never seen alive again. Several days later his 1975 Chevy Impala was found in the parking lot of the

Miami airport with his golf clubs still in the trunk. Eleven days after his disappearance a couple of fishermen found a 55 gallon drum floating in the bay. It was wrapped in chains with holes drilled into it. Through the holes, the men saw the swollen, decaying body of Johnny Roselli. It seemed that the killer perhaps had attached weights that had broken off and the gases in the decomposing body kept it afloat. To this day, no one has confirmed who killed Roselli. Today, there are only theories and the murder remains a mystery, but then again, mystery is what Miami is all about.

The Devil's Triangle

"It is the strange fate of man, that even in the greatest of evils the fear of the worst continues to haunt him." ~ *Johann Wolgang Von Goethe*

Many believe that certain areas are haunted or have unusual energy associated with them due to their location. Water seems to be a factor. Like New Orleans, Miami is surrounded by water. But on top of that, Miami is located on the tip of one of the three corners of the Bermuda Triangle, one of the world's most powerful energy vortices. Regardless of what causes the energy changes in the triangle, it has a direct effect on Miami.

Often referred to as the Graveyard of the Atlantic, the Bermuda Triangle is situated at the Northwest edge of Bermuda, the Southwest edge of San Juan, Puerto Rico, and the Northeast edge of Miami, Florida. It goes by many names including the Devil's Triangle, Limbo of the Lost, Hoodoo Sea, and the Twilight Zone. It covers approximately 500,000 square miles of the Atlantic Ocean.

In the past one hundred years, more than fifty boats and twenty aircraft have mysteriously disappeared in the triangle, never to be seen again. Most of them vanished without a trace. Just prior to disappearing, crews have made radio contact indicating no problems. In some instances, missing ships have been found without their crews and passengers.

Many theories have been presented through the years ranging from alien abductions to vortices that lead to a fourth dimension. More scientific explanations exist. There seems to be an abnormal magnetic field present in the area. Compasses usually point magnetic north allowing for up to twenty degrees in variances depending on the location. In the triangle compasses show true north. Another factor is the Gulf Stream present in the triangle which is swift and treacherous. Unpredictable weather patterns in the Atlantic and Caribbean are also taken into consideration. Sudden storms and waterspouts can spring out of nowhere spelling disaster for ships and aircraft. Christopher Columbus wrote of seeing a great fire in the sky that crashed into the sea during his voyage through the triangle. Shortly before his famous landing, he wrote of seeing strange lights in the sky and abnormal compass readings. Then in 1892, the ship *Mary Celeste* was found 400 miles off its intended course. Her crew was never found.

The triangle was named in 1945 after the disappearance of six navy planes and their crews on December 5. It was a sunny day, ideal for flying. Commander Lt. Charles Taylor was leading a group of trainees on a routine flight. The mission called for the team to fly due east 56 miles to conduct practice bombing runs. The team would then fly another 67 miles east then turn north for 73 miles and straight back to the base. The course took them on a triangular route over the sea.

About an hour and a half into the flight, radio transmissions were picked up from Taylor who indicated that his compasses were not working but he believed himself to be somewhere over the Keys. Lt. Robert Cox instructed him to fly north toward Miami. The disoriented Taylor made futile attempts to fly into Miami but continued to fly further out to sea. By 4:45 PM, he was hopelessly lost. Communication died as it grew dark. At 6:30 PM, a Dumbo Flying Boat was dispatched to find Flight 19. Two hours later, two more planes, Martin Mariners, joined the search. The search continued throughout the night and into the next day. Flight 19 and one of the Martin Mariners had disappeared.

Other disappearances include the *Marine Sulphur Queen* that had made sixty-three voyages prior to disappearing in the triangle. After several days of searching for the ship, all that was found were a few life jackets, life rings, and some debris. On page 224 of Martin Caidin's book, *Ghosts of the Air*, he reported that a National Airlines Boeing 727 disappeared from the radar on its final approach to Miami International Airport. Helicopters searched for wreckage assuming the plane crashed on approach but nothing was ever found. Ten minutes after its disappearance, the 727 reappeared in the exact same location it had vanished just moments before. The plane landed as normal with no mishaps. The Captain and crew had no knowledge of the disappearance but when they landed their aircraft clocks and watches were ten minutes behind ground time as if time stood still for them.

Perhaps the strange magnetic pull that the triangle possesses has something to do with the unusual energy felt in the Miami area. A strong pulling sensation can be felt in South Beach, as if being pulled towards the ocean. It may also have an effect on the minds and behavior of those in that area. This at first might seem a little farfetched, but take into consideration what happens with changes in the moon in relationship to the earth. Just as the moon affects the tides, it also affects animals and humans both physically and mentally.

I have spoken to various medical personnel at hospitals and nursing homes. Most agree that emergency surgeries and illnesses increase during a full moon. One nursing home employee reported that staff members fight over who will work on a full moon because no wants that overnight shift.

He told me that there was a significant increase in not only accidents and illnesses but sudden death on the night of a full moon.

The "Lunar Effect" suggests that the full moon indeed has a profound effect on human behavior. The word *lunatic* stems from the word *luna* meaning moon in Latin. Many people do seem to behave strangely during the full moon. One theory is that the hypothalamus gland is affected during this time causing changes in moods and emotions. Changes in the hypothalamus would produce chemical imbalances in the brain affecting changes in behavior. It is entirely possible that the variances in the energetic and magnetic field in the triangle could have the same effect physiologically. This might explain the extreme violence and murder common in the Miami area.

Crimes of Passion

"Every murder turns on a bright hot light, and a lot of people... have to walk out of the shadows." ~ *Albert Maltz*

A large percentage of Miami's murders wind up being murder/suicides, often involving the elderly. Being a favorite retirement spot, there is a large population of older citizens which might account for this. Although not all of these crimes involve retirees, a vast majority do. Most leave no explanation as to the reason. One couple went from the altar to the funeral home in a matter of days.

On April 4, 1999, a fifty-four-year-old real estate broker married his long-time girlfriend. The marriage was her fourth and his third. Only eight days after the wedding, the bride filed for divorce. But rather than try to reconcile his short-lived marriage, the new groom slit her throat then drove to a local funeral home and blew his brains out in the parking lot. Her nude body was found in a pool of blood inside their home along with his suicide note.

Of all the murder/suicides in Miami, none was more shocking than the one that ended its tragic saga at Casa Casuarina. The Casa was built in 1930 by architect, Alden Freeman as homage to the oldest existing house in the Western Hemisphere, "Alcazar de Colon" in Santo Domingo. The Alcazar was home to Christopher Columbus' son, Diego, in 1510. The Casa's cornerstone even contained an original brick from the Alcazar. In 1937, after Freeman's death, the house was purchased by Jacques Amsterdam who renamed it the Amsterdam Palace. In 1992, designer Gianni Versace encountered the Casa while visiting Miami and fell in love with it. The mansion became his primary residence.

Andrew Cunanan was a party boy in San Diego's gay scene. He was described by friends as handsome, charming, and intelligent, but his mother described him as simply a high class male prostitute who enjoyed a life of luxuries. His high school class named him "least likely to be forgotten."

Cunanan's cross-country murderous rampage began on April 29, 1997 when police discovered the body of Jeffrey Trail rolled in a carpet in the apartment of Cunanan's former lover, Minneapolis architect David Madson. Trail's answering machine contained a message from Cunanan inviting him to Madson's apartment. Four days later, David Madson's body was found near a lake. He had multiple gunshot wounds.

The next victim was Chicago millionaire, Lee Miglin, 72, who was found wrapped in plastic in his garage. He had been stabbed and slashed numerous times. After the murder, the killer allegedly made himself a ham sandwich and shaved with the dead man's razor. Police found Madson's red jeep Cherokee parked at the home. Miglin's green 1994 Lexus was missing. The Lexus reappeared on May 9 in a Pennsville, New Jersey cemetery along with the body of a caretaker, William Reese, 45, who had been shot in the head. After shooting Reese, Cunanan stole his red 1995 Chevy pickup truck.

On July 23, Cunanan appeared on the doorstep of Casa Casuarina and fatally shot Gianni Versace at point blank range in the head. After leaving Versace dying on his doorstep, Cunanan walked away leaving a pile of bloody clothing in a nearby parking lot along with the vehicle he had stolen from his previous victim. More than 400 FBI agents along with citizen vigilantes scoured Miami Beach in search for Cunanan. The drama ended on July 23 when Cunanan's lifeless body was found in a two-story boathouse two and a half miles from the Versace home. Cunanan's final victim was himself having blown his own face off. He left no suicide note.

Obviously, Andrew Cunanan's odyssey of carnage leading to his suicide cannot be blamed on anything other than his own mental sickness. But it is curious that his trail of death leading to his own demise ended in Miami. Not all murders of the rich and famous end in suicide. One of the most infamous murder cases in Miami was that of a wealthy banker.

Candace Weatherby was only in her twenties when she launched a successful modeling agency and finishing school in New Orleans. She volunteered in her spare time as a fundraiser for the New Orleans Grand Opera Company. This position put her in front of some of the most affluent people in the city including banker, Jacques Mossler.

Mossler owned a bank in New Orleans and met Candace in the fall of 1948 when she solicited him for a donation. After several months of dating, the couple married and moved to Houston, Texas. They adopted four children who had been orphaned. The family lived a lavish lifestyle in the posh River Oaks section of Houston.

In 1956, Candace's brother, DeWitt Weatherby killed a man during a poker game and was sentenced to life in prison. Candace sweet talked her husband into spending a fortune on political favors in order to buy her brother's parole. DeWitt was released on parole five years later. Then in 1961, another destitute family member appeared on the scene in need of help, Candace's nephew, Melvin Powers. Melvin was her sister's son. He had recently been released from prison on fraud charges. He was only twenty-years-old. Once again, Candace used her feminine wiles to convince her husband to help Melvin. Mossler hired the young man to work in one of his financial institutes in Houston. Melvin moved in with the family and enjoyed his new life of wealth and prestige.

Jacques Mossler fell ill with a respiratory disease in 1962 requiring frequent trips to Europe for treatments. That's when the unfathomable happened. Candace Mossler began an incestuous affair with her nephew! An ailing Jacques Mossler began to spend more time away from the Houston home, opting for a posh apartment in Miami for health reasons. All the while Jacques was convalescing, his wife carried on a torrid love affair with Melvin.

Eventually whispers of incest and betrayal made their way to Jacques' ears. Too ashamed to face society in Houston, he retreated to his Miami home. Melvin was fired from the company and forced to move from the Mossler home. But that didn't stop "Aunt Candy" from visiting him. She moved the family to Miami and continued to make frequent trips to spend time with her lover.

Once in Miami, Candace developed frequent migraine headaches requiring midnight trips to the emergency room. She would take all of the Mossler children to the hospital returning home hours later. On one of those visits, she returned to find her husband's lifeless body with thirty-nine stab wounds.

Eye witnesses and airline records proved that Melvin Powers had flown into Miami just hours before the murder, then departed shortly thereafter, returning to Houston. A car belonging to Candace had been abandoned in the airport parking lot. Traces of blood and Melvin's fingerprints were found in the vehicle. A witness identified the car as having been seen at the home the evening of the murder. Jacques Mossler's diary indicated that he feared his wife and Melvin might kill him. With compelling evidence, the DA set out to prosecute Candace Mossler and Melvin Powers for first degree murder.

Some say crime doesn't pay but it seemed to have this time. Jacques Mossler might have been gone but his fortune was not. Candace used his money to hire attorneys for their defense. After a very public and scandalous trial, a jury found both Candace and Melvin not guilty. The couple went their separate ways after the trial. Candace Mossler died in 1976 in the Fontainebleau Hotel in Miami from complications of a migraine treatment. While Candace Mossler escaped justice for murdering her husband, twenty-two years later, another discontent wife of a millionaire committed what has been called the imperfect crime.

Joyce Lemay moved to Miami in her early twenties after a sad and unstable childhood in rural Illinois. The daughter of alcoholic parents, she spent most of life living as a gypsy with her unemployed mother. She endured physical and sexual abuse in various foster homes and orphanages. By the time she was seventeen-years-old, she was married and had a son. Five years into the marriage, in 1973, Joyce convinced her husband to find work in Miami, Florida. Within a year, her husband returned to Illinois without Joyce. In fall 1974, Joyce secured a secretarial position with a successful construction firm, SAC Construction owned by Stanley Cohen. Sixteen years her senior, he became immediately smitten with the twenty-four-year-old Joyce. The two were married that same year just weeks after her divorce had become official.

It didn't take Joyce long to become accustomed to the good life. Stanley bought her a mansion in Miami's prestigious Coconut Grove neighborhood. He paid for her to attend school in interior design, and lavished her with gifts. She eventually persuaded him to buy a second home in the mountains of Colorado. He even purchased a private plane to transport them to and from the mountain lodge. As time went on, Joyce spent more and more time away from Miami, developing her own social circle in Colorado.

Needless to say, the distance between the two took its toll on their intimacy and Stanley began an affair with a former girlfriend. Drugs, infidelity, and arguments dominated the marriage. When Joyce threatened to leave Stanley he reminded her that she would leave with what she came with, which was nothing. Joyce enjoyed her husband's wealth and the social status it afforded her. Somewhere along the line, eleven years into the marriage, she decided that if anyone was going to leave with nothing, it would be Stanley.

On March 7, 1986, a call came in to 911 at 5:25 AM. That call came from the Cohens' Coconut Grove Mansion. The caller was Joyce Cohen reporting that her husband had been shot. The police arrived on the scene to find the nude body of Stanley Cohen in bed with a fatal gunshot to the head. Joyce told police that she had fallen asleep downstairs and was awakened to a gunshot. She described seeing two men fleeing from the home as she ran towards the stairs. Finding no sign of robbery, police became suspicious.

Within an hour of the investigation, Joyce demanded that the police obtain a search warrant. As they waited outside, police found a .38 revolver belonging to Stanley hidden in a fern pot. When questioned later, Joyce explained that she had heard something outside earlier that evening and sent Stanley out to investigate. She went on to say that

Stanley must have left the gun on the nightstand and the intruders used it to kill him. Later it was discovered that neighbors heard the shots at 3 AM, the same time of death determined by the coroner. Joyce did not call 911 until almost two and a half hours later.

After a lengthy investigation and trial, it was revealed that Joyce had hired hit men to kill Stanley. She paid them $100,000.00 worth of cocaine to commit the murder. Joyce Cohen was convicted of first degree murder and sentenced to life in prison. She lost all rights to any of the Cohen fortune.

A more recent death that brought Miami into the spotlight involved the infamous Fontainebleau Hotel. This time it was the owner of the hotel who was murdered.

In April 2009 eighty-seven-year-old Bernice Novack was found bludgeoned to death in her home in Fort Lauderdale. Her jaw had been broken and the walls of her home covered in blood. Mrs. Novack was the widow of the late Ben Novack, Sr., founder of the Fontainebleau Hotel in Miami Beach. At first authorities believed that she had fallen but it was later determined that she had been beaten to death. Three months later, the body of her son, Ben Novack, Jr. was found in a New York hotel. Someone had murdered him.

On that July morning in 2009, Ben Novack Jr. and his wife, Narcy, were staying in a suburban hotel in Rye Brook, New York. Initially, Narcy made the call telling authorities that she had gone to breakfast and returned to find her husband dead. Authorities later learned that it was Narcy who opened the hotel room door and allowed the killers to gain entry. It was also she who offered a pillow to one of the three killers to muffle the screams of her husband as he was bound and beaten with a dumbbell. She watched as Ben's eyes were cut out. The motive was money. The day after the murder, Narcy stole $100,000.00 from Ben's business.

There were rumors that Ben was having an affair and possibly considering divorcing Narcy, his wife of nineteen years. Narcy, a former stripper, wasn't about to lose her lifestyle or inheritance for any other woman. Narcy and her brother, Cristobal Veliz, scouted the hotel one week before the murder to make plans for the attack. Veliz returned on July 9 with two accomplices to take care of business. The accomplices confessed that they killed Novack at the direction of his wife and that she paid them for the murder. Today Narcy Novack sits in prison awaiting trial for her husband's murder and six other felony counts. Like Joyce Cohen, Narcy Novack lost all rights to any inheritance.

Serial Killers

"I am a serial killer. I would kill again." ~ Aileen Wuornos

Some people kill for money. Some people kill for love. Some kill out of self-defense or to protect a loved one. But what makes a person kill over and over again without provocation? Serial killers are the worst of all murderers. They have no motive, no incentive, other than they enjoy killing for sport.

What goes on in the minds of these human monsters that drives them to destroy the lives of others?

The psychopath forms no emotional attachment to anyone. They abuse, even kill others with no remorse, no guilt. The true psychopath has no empathy for others, they feel no shame. According to many biographies of serial killers, a large percentage of them suffered traumatic childhoods filled with abuse. Many of them lived as social outcasts and misfits often isolating themselves from others.

According to FBI statistics, most serial killers are white males between the ages of twenty and forty-years-old. Many of them have a history of cruel behavior towards other humans and animals. Most serial killers seem to choose their victims randomly often targeting those who are most vulnerable such as prostitutes, vagrants, drug addicts, or runaways.

Forensic psychiatrist, John Marshall Macdonald noted in an article in 1963 in the American Journal of Psychiatry, "The Threat to Kill," a triad of characteristics in children that he believed predicted sociopathic behavior. The triad of sociopathy, also called the Macdonald Triad, is a history of bedwetting, starting fires, and torturing animals. Animal torture seems to be the biggest red flag. Cannibal serial killer, Jeffrey Dahmer, killed and beheaded dogs as a child.

In a study conducted by the University of Wisconsin School of Medicine, doctors suggested that brain function in psychopaths are different from normal people. The study proved that the psychopathic brain has reduced connections between the ventromedial prefrontal cortex, which controls empathy and guilt, and the amygdala, the part of the brain responsible for fear and anxiety.

Charles Henry Williams was raised in poverty in the ghetto of Miami. A drug addict, he used drugs in exchange for sex to lure prostitutes into remote areas. Each victim was found face down, legs spread apart, and strangled. Most of them had high amounts of cocaine in their system at the time of death.

The bodies were usually found in vacant lots, in stairwells, and near dumpsters. Although he never admitted to any of the murders, it's believed that he killed at least thirty-two women between 1984 and 1989.

Due to lack of evidence, Williams was convicted for only one of the murders. He still insists that he did not kill the other women.

Many serial killers kill in a ritualistic fashion as in the case of the Tamiami Strangler, Rory Conde. His mother died when he was only six months old. Rory spent the first twelve years of his life with his grandmother in Columbia then moved to Miami to live with his father. He married at twenty-one and became an abusive husband and father. Carla Conde, his wife of seven years, later told authorities that he beat her frequently and threatened her with guns. She believed that Conde's father may have abused him as a child.

Conde indulged himself with prostitutes frequently. He made the mistake of bringing one of them home and videotaped her masturbating on his bed, wearing his wife's lingerie. Carla discovered the tape and left him, taking their child with her. The couple later reconciled and moved to a condominium located on the Tamiami Trail. Conde's behavior began to change as soon as his wife became pregnant again.

He frequently disappeared on mysterious overnight "fishing trips." His wife never saw any evidence that he had actually been fishing. She did notice unusual scratches on his back. When she questioned him about the scratches, he beat her mercilessly. The final straw for Carla was having caught him masturbating while peeping into a neighbor's window. She took both children and left. Conde threatened to kill her if she dated anyone.

Once on his own, Conde continued to pursue prostitutes despite blaming them for his wife's departure. On September 15, 1994 he picked up a prostitute for oral sex on the Tamiami Trail. The hooker turned out to be a transsexual. According to his confession later given to authorities, Conde strangled his victim dumping the body in nearby residential neighborhood. Five other murders followed over the next four months. All of the victims were strangled, redressed, and dumped in obvious locations.

Conde was caught on June 19, 1995 when neighbors reported strange sounds coming from his apartment. Police found a prostitute bound by duct tape struggling to free herself. Conde was eventually convicted for six murders and given the death penalty.

One Miami serial killer was never captured. Between 2000 and 2007 the bodies of six women were found inside containers and dumped near major thoroughfares. Three identified victims were crammed into suitcases giving the unknown killer the nickname, the Suitcase Murderer. Those not found in suitcases were shoved into plastic containers. Like many of the other victims of serial killers, the women were prostitutes addicted to drugs and alcohol. As of 2007, the Miami-Dade County P.D. reported a total of fourteen unsolved murders of prostitutes including those believed to be part of the suitcase murders.

Christopher Wilder was a sexual predator who posed as a photographer to lure young girls to his home or remote locations for modeling sessions. His lust drove him to molesting numerous girls and young women. In1974 he was arrested for rape. He enticed a girl in a shopping mall to follow him to his vehicle. The girl was forced inside, where he drugged and raped her. He set the girl free and she went to the police. He was tried for the rape but somehow managed to escape imprisonment being put on probation and requiring sex therapy.

Neither court nor therapy was new to Wilder. At seventeen he was convicted for gang rape in his native Australian town, and received probation along with counseling and electroshock therapy. Wilder eventually left Australia taking up residence in South Florida where he found a suitable job. A thrill-seeker, Wilder took up race car driving as a hobby as well as photography.

On March 4, 1984, Elizabeth Kenyon, a twenty-three-year-old teacher, had spent the day visiting her parents in Pompano Beach. At about 9:00 PM she departed heading back to her apartment in Coral Gables. She never made it home. Several days later, her car was found parked at the airport. This was the second disappearance in Miami in less than a month. On February 26, twenty-year-old Rosaria Gonzales had also vanished without a trace.

Within a few days, the police found a connection between the two disappearances. Both women knew Christopher Wilder. Elizabeth Kenyon had dated Wilder for a while. He even proposed marriage but Kenyon felt he was too old for her so she declined the proposal but remained friends with him. Rosaria Gonzales knew Wilder from the race track they both frequented. The search for Wilder began.

On March 23, the body of Terry Ferguson, an aspiring model, was found in a canal. Terry had been missing for five days. Witnesses described seeing her with a man fitting Wilder's description the day she disappeared.

By now Wilder was on the run. His next victim was a nineteen-year-old female that he met in a shopping mall in Tallahassee. He approached her offering her twenty dollars an hour for a modeling session. He told her she need only go with him to a local park. When the girl declined his offer, he punched her in the stomach and dragged her into his car. Shortly thereafter, in a remote area, he stopped and covered her mouth with duct tape and bound her arms and legs. He then forced her into the trunk.

Wilder drove all the way to Georgia, eventually checking into a small motel where he beat, tortured, and raped her repeatedly. In an attempt to prevent her from seeing him, he used super glue on her eyelids and a blow dryer to dry them shut. He then attached wires to her feet that were attached to an electrical device that he used to shock her feet. The girl somehow managed to fight him off and locked herself in the bathroom where she screamed and beat on the walls. Wilder quickly packed up and left the scene. Once he left the room, the girl covered herself with a sheet and staggered to the motel office where authorities were called. The girl identified a photo of Wilder as her attacker.

By April 3, three more young women disappeared across the South and Central U.S. Wilder was now on the F.B.I.'s most wanted list. His victims were all beautiful young women who could pass as models giving Wilder the nickname The Beauty Queen

Killer. Wilder was in a frenzy. He drove all the way to California then back across the country to New York, leaving a trail of dead women along the way. By April 13, he had added four more victims to the count. On that Friday the 13th, his luck ran out.

He tried to abduct a nineteen-year-old from a highway in Beverly, Massachusetts, where her car had broken down. She got into the car with Wilder but when he passed up the gas station, she realized something was wrong. She asked him to pull over but Wilder pulled a gun on her instead. The girl managed to open the car door and jumped out. Wilder sped away heading for New Hampshire. There he stopped at a gas station and state police recognized him.

The troopers got out of their car and called out to Wilder who immediately jumped into his car. One of the troopers jumped in behind him right on Wilder's back. As Wilder struggled for his gun and the trooper tried to stop him, Wilder fired twice. One shot went into the trooper, the other shot Wilder in the chest killing him instantly. The trail of death ended at his own hand.

As heinous as the crimes of Christopher Wilder, his sins paled in comparison to another serial killer who plagued South Florida during the same time. Wilder's rampage was over but another more fiendish monster and his deranged sidekick were still at large. Only these vicious killers not only murdered their victims, they ate them.

Two of the deadliest and most sadistic killers in American history teamed up in Miami and worked together in a free-wheeling killing spree that terrorized South Florida for years. Their deadly alliance left a trail of death across the entire Southern United States.

The Devil Made Them Do It

"Once I've done a crime, I just forget it. I go from crime to crime." ~ Henry Lee Lucas

Deep in the Everglades a pact was made with the devil. Those who worshipped the Prince of Darkness gathered together on a small island to prepare for their next ritual. Two newcomers were to be initiated into the cult. They are taken by airboat, their eyes covered by blindfold, to the appointed infernal location. The two men were led to their tents and told to wait for instructions.

Moments later the mysterious leader appeared again and told them, "From now on, you will do everything you are told, without question. You will be told to kill someone while you are here and you will obey. Once you have proven yourself, you will be one of us."

The men were led to another tent and told to slit the throat of the man inside. They entered the tent. Both of them had killed before. Both of them killed for the enjoyment of it. They were introduced to the younger man and they enticed him to the shoreline for a drink. When he tossed his head back to take a sip of whiskey one of the initiates grabbed him by the hair and slit his throat from ear to ear. The initiates laughed with delight at the sight of blood and whiskey as it gushed from his throat. The two took the body and delivered it to the leader.

The body was then put on a table in the middle of a large tent. The members gathered around as the leader cut the dead man's heart out, and drained his blood. A cup of blood was passed around for all to drink as they dismembered the body. Some parts of the body were cooked and eaten by the congregation. The remainder was burned on the altar as a sacrifice to Satan.

This is what took place during an initiation into a nationwide satanic cult called "The Hand of Death." This is according to serial killers Ottis Toole and Henry Lee Lucas. In David McGowan's *Programmed to Kill*, Lucas told police, "They take a live girl and put her on the table and split her open and take all of her organs out."

He went on to explain that entrails were taken then cooked in a pot and eaten by the members.

Max Call in his book, *Hand of Death*, The Henry Lee Lucas Story, writes, "There were several hundred students at the Hand of Death training camp, coming from six different countries; over half of them were women. The camp provided unlimited access to all kinds of drug taking, which was encouraged recreational activity. Liquor was available, and after evening ritualistic sacrifices, there would be an orgy involving all of the campers."

The Hand of Death camp was never located. Some authorities thought that the pair of psychopaths made up the story. What they knew was true was that both of these men collectively killed over two hundred people. They killed individually and as a duo. They killed for sport. If demonic forces do exist in this world, no doubt it's what brought these two together.

Ottis Toole was born in Jacksonville, Florida in 1947. Abandoned by his father, he grew up with his mother, sister, and grandmother. His mother often dressed him as a girl when he went to school. He was a misfit who was commonly mistreated by the other children. He quit school in the fifth grade. Later IQ tests would reveal that in addition to having severe learning disabilities, ADD, and dyslexia, Ottis Toole's IQ was below seventy.

His grandmother labeled him "The Devil's Child." She worshipped the devil and participated in Satanic Rituals bringing young Ottis along with her. He accompanied his grandmother in grave robbing for body parts for her rituals. By the time he was in his teens, Ottis ran away frequently and acted out his abuse by burning down abandoned buildings. He made money as a male prostitute, usually dressing in drag.

Ottis confessed that his first murder occurred when he was only fourteen-years-old. A man picked him up for sex and drove to a wooded area. After sex, Ottis ran over him with his own car. Police were never able to verify the murder.

Otis was twenty-nine-years-old in 1976 when he met forty-year-old Henry Lee Lucas in a soup kitchen in Jacksonville. Having so much in common the two instantly became friends and eventually lovers. They spent the next few years travelling from state to state stealing and killing every step of the way.

Henry Lee Lucas was the youngest of eight children born to poverty stricken alcoholic parents. His father had lost his legs when hit by a train many years before. His mother, Viola, was a prostitute and bootlegger who lived not only with her husband and children but her pimp. Henry Lee was forced as a child to watch his mother "entertain" her clients.

Viola Lucas was an abusive woman who mistreated her children and crippled husband. Henry Lee's father's life seemed to revolve around the family still. He was an alcoholic by age ten. Like Ottis, Henry Lee's mother frequently dressed him as a girl. When he was five, Viola hit him in the head with a board causing future blackouts and seizures.

Viola's pimp, Bernie, introduced Henry Lee to bestiality and necrophilia. In his teens, Henry Lee had sex with the carcasses of mutilated dogs and sheep. He committed his first murder when he was fifteen. He killed a girl because he wanted to see what it was like to have sex with a human. Henry Lee spent the rest of his life preferring sex with corpses rather than living humans. Henry admitted to authorities many years later, "...to me a live woman ain't nothin'. I enjoy dead sex more than I do live sex."

In 1960 during a drunken argument with his mother, Henry Lee plunged a knife into her chest killing her. He then raped the corpse. He was convicted and sent to a penitentiary in Michigan but soon got transferred to a psychiatric facility after attempting suicide. There he was diagnosed a suicidal psychopath. He was given four years of counseling and electroshock therapy then sent back to prison. He was released on parole after serving only ten years of the twenty year sentence. He then spent more time in prison for attempting to kidnap two girls. Eventually, he was released again and made his way to South Florida where he met Ottis.

Henry Lee and Ottis moved in together living with some of Ottis' family which included a young niece and nephew. Henry Lee and Ottis continued on killing sprees through 1983. They shot their victims, stabbed them, hanged them, raped and dismembered them. Then Ottis would dispose of the body by cutting it up and cooking it. He described to a reporter in detail how he delighted in cooking and eating human flesh.

He told one reporter, "...you strip them naked and hang them upside by their ankles; then you slit their throat with a knife, slit the belly and take out the guts, the liver, and the heart. Cut off the head. Let the blood drain. I use a pit. A barbeque pit.

Charcoal so there ain't much smoke. Take down the body, put the metal spit through them. Put it into the asshole, through the body, and out the neck…and put it on the spit holder over the coals. Damn tasty."

Ottis went on to describe the taste of young children as tasting like "roast pig." He told the reporter, "Some people eat pigs, cows, horses. I like to eat people. It's good meat too. You ain't tried it, don't you be saying it ain't tasty. You might like it."

Ottis had a particular taste for male genitalia. He described to a reporter what he did with the bodies used in the rituals. He told the reporter, "…cut off the peter, cut off the balls, and it's put in like a little stew pot."

He further explained, "The balls are damn good when fried. Use a little batter and fryer and it's a real treat. Fresh fried balls is one of my favorites…"

Cooking the victims solved two problems for the killers, evidence and hunger. If the bodies were cut up, cooked, and eaten, there is no body of evidence. If they ate their victims, they were assured that they'd never have to spend time in a soup kitchen again.

At some point in time, they met a man called Don Meteric who allegedly introduced them to The Hand of Death Cult in Miami. Some believe that possibly Meteric knew Ottis from his grandmother who belonged to a Satanic Cult. Others believe the pair made up the cult. They did say that most of the cult's activity besides a training camp in Miami was along the Texas-Mexico border. They swore that they were paid to kidnap young women and children and bring them to Mexico to be used in rituals. Officials could never find any evidence that the cult existed at that time.

The pair disconnected from Meteric in 1981 when Ottis' mother and sister died. His niece and nephew, Becky and Frank Powell, were left in a foster home. Ottis and Henry Lee returned to Florida rescuing the kids and taking them along on their adventures. Before long, Henry Lee developed a relationship with Becky who was mildly retarded and only twelve-years-old at the time. Ottis began to feel betrayed by Henry Lee and eventually the two parted company. Becky went with Henry Lee.

Outraged at the betrayal by his lover, Ottis went on a rampage. He was arrested in 1983 on charges of murder and arson in Florida. A psychiatric evaluation done in prison provided some insight to the damage in Ottis' brain. He suffered from severe frontal neurological damage and was considered incapable of controlling his impulses. Diagnosed as mentally retarded, illiterate, and a drug addict, Ottis was deemed unable to premeditate his actions. Meanwhile, Henry Lee and Becky travelled to Texas.

The couple found refuge in the unlikely setting of a Pentecostal commune. Becky soon became homesick for Florida and demanded Henry Lee take her back. Henry agreed but told her they would have to hitchhike back. He took her out on an open road near a field. The two argued about her going home.

Henry Lee lost his temper and stabbed the girl in the heart. He then had sex with her corpse before cutting her up in pieces and dispersing parts of her around the field. He returned without her to the commune. When questioned by an older woman on Becky's whereabouts, he stabbed her to death too. After having sex with her corpse, he shoved it into a drainage ditch.

He left the commune for about a month only to return to the drainage ditch and retrieve the body he had left there. He attempted to bring it to the church incinerator and burn it. Realizing he was a suspect in the woman's disappearance, and the disappearance of Becky, he ultimately confessed to the murders. In jail, he wrote a letter to Ottis. He admitted to him what he had done to Becky and told Ottis that he wanted him to assist him on remembering details on all the murders they had committed.

Although authorities were hard pressed to believe the number of people the two had murdered, after speaking with both men, they realized that it would have been impossible for them to fabricate such details having not seen each other in months.

Lucas confessed to three hundred sixty murders. He later recanted saying he lied and the only person he killed was his mother and that had been an accident. Then he went back to saying he did kill the people he said he had. No one really knows how many he actually killed and how many he lied about. Few believe either Henry Lee or Ottis were smart enough to fabricate intricate details that they had. While serving several life sentences, Henry Lee died of natural causes in 2001.

Ottis Toole confessed to hundreds of murders. He detailed not only how the victims were killed but enjoyed retelling how the bodies were cut, cooked, and eaten. One of the murders he confessed was that of Adam Walsh, a six-year-old who disappeared from a Hollywood, Florida shopping mall in 1981. The child's head was found in a nearby canal but his body never recovered. Like Henry Lee, Ottis confessed then recanted, then went back and forth again.

Police botched the original investigation into the Walsh murder by losing significant evidence. Ottis Toole died of cirrhosis of the liver in 1997 while in prison. But in 2008 it was determined that Ottis was indeed Adam's killer.

The Hand of Death Cult was never verified. But in 1988, authorities found a mass grave at a ranch in Matamoros, Mexico, just miles from Brownsville, Texas. Along with the bodies of a dozen people was evidence of Satanic rituals and human sacrifices. Among the dead was a twenty-one-year-old University of Texas student, Mark Kilroy, who had apparently been recently sacrificed in a ritual. It was later determined that a drug smuggling Satanic cult led by Adolfo de Jesus Constanzo was to blame.

Constanzo was born in Miami on November 1, 1962. He was only six months old when his fifteen-year-old Cuban mother took him to be blessed by a priest of Palo Mayombe, a powerful form of magic originated in the Congo. She became convinced that her child was the "chosen one." By the time he was ten-years-old, he was in full apprenticeship of the priest learning the darker side of magic.

Over the next several years, his mother was arrested over thirty times for everything from shoplifting to grand theft and child neglect. She always managed to regain her freedom without serving time or probation. She credited the magic of her religion for her ability to escape punishment. She and Aldolfo moved from house to house. When neighbors accused the young mother of being a witch, she would leave headless animals on their doorsteps.

As a young adult, Constanzo frequented the Miami gay bars and committed petty crimes. He continued studying under the priest, robbing graves, and spilling blood over dolls to curse enemies. During this time, he began a career as a drug dealer.

Later called El Padrino de Matamoros (The Godfather of Matamoros) he rose to the ranks of leader of a Satanic Cult and drug lord in a drug dealing operation that spread from Miami into Mexico. In 1984, he left Miami and settled in Mexico City where he made a legitimate living as a tarot card reader and brujo (witch). He sold magic spells, offered cleanses to clients to remove curses, some of which he charged thousands of dollars to perform. He offered high priced rituals to drug dealers to make them invisible to police. It was there that he met Martín Quintana Rodríguez and Omar Chewe Orea Ochoa who became his closest disciples and lovers. He eventually set up a base camp at a ranch in Matamoros, Mexico.

Because most of his activities were South of the border, few details are known about what went on at that ranch. It is believed that prior to his death in 1989, he and his followers were responsible for numerous ritual deaths, which included children and teenagers kidnapped along the Texas border. Most of his victims were Mexican citizens hoping to cross the border or simple drug dealers.

In May, 1987, seven mutilated bodies of a rival drug family were found in the Zumpango River in Mexico. Fingers, toes, ears, hearts, and sex organs had been removed from all of them. Two were missing brains, and one was missing part of his spine. It could never be proven whether Constanzo committed the murders. The elusive godfather continued to live underground in various hideouts throughout Mexico.

In April, 1989 Mexican officials and U.S. Border Patrol authorities made the gruesome discovery. Of the twelve bodies found buried on the ranch, some had been shot, some chopped with a machete, but all were missing brains. Among the evidence found nearby the gravesite were candles, animal bones, and a blood filled cauldron containing spiders, scorpions, a dead black cat, a turtle shell, bones, deer antlers, and a human brain. All of the dead were males most of whom were local drug smugglers, except that of Mark Kilroy. Mark had gone out for a night of drinking in Matamoros with friends on March 14. A short time after 2:00 AM, he disappeared.

Four suspects were arrested, all of whom named Constanzo as their godfather in the cult. In their confessions, the suspects told police that Constanzo ordered them to find one Anglo male to sacrifice. They then told police that Constanzo killed him with a chopping blow of a machete to the back of his neck. The brains of all of the victims were eaten by the cult members after the ritual.

Police finally cornered Constanzo in Mexico City on May 6. Determined not to be arrested, Constanzo ordered one of his minions to shoot him before police could get to him. By the time police had knocked the door down, Constanzo was dead.

There was never a connection made between Constanzo's cult and the Hand of Death that Henry Lee Lucas and Ottis Toole swore existed. It's very likely the two were one in the same as both began in Miami and ended in a border town in Mexico.

It should be noted that these murderers, despite the fact that they claimed to be worshippers of Satan, are not representing what is considered true Satanism. The real Satanic church, a bonafide religion, was established in the 1960s by Anton LaVey in San Francisco. In his Satanic Bible, LaVey admits that he does not recognize a deity called God, nor does he believe in the Devil. The church uses Satan and his fallen angels as metaphors for the human persona. Satanism is more accurately Humanism. There are no outside deities; practitioners believe that gods and devils reside within. It is the worship of the self.

A Satanic priest, Thomas Mack, explained that many of the actions in a ritual are purely symbolic. There are no wild sex orgies, nor human sacrifices. Because they do not worship any outside deity, they make no sacrifices to one. He explained that those individuals who use the religion as an excuse for their activities are simply criminals not willing to accept responsibility for their crimes. They use the religion as an excuse to kill.

Not all cult murderers are killing because they worship Satan. In fact, a great number of them claim that they commit crime in the name of God, Himself.

For God's Sake

"From fanaticism to barbarism is only one step." ~ Denis Diderot

Killers come from all walks of life. Every religion has its share of criminals within. This holds true in Voodoo and Santeria communities as well. Both religions are very prevalent in Miami. Santeria is practiced in the Cuban communities and Voodoo is practiced amongst the Haitians. The religions are extremely similar as both made their way into the Caribbean via the slave trade from Africa. Voodoo originated in the Dahomey region, now Benin, travelling into Haiti. Santeria finds its root in the Yoruba tradition, stemming from Nigeria. Although different languages are present, the concept remains the same. Both believe in one God the creator and many deities created by that God who work on behalf of the practitioners on a day to day basis. In Voodoo, these spirits are the Lwa. In Santeria, they are called Orishas. In both religions, each deity has a specific purpose much like the Catholic Saints.

The most powerful and commonly used Orishas are called Las Sietas Potencia Africanas (The Seven African Powers). These spirits are called upon in both Voodoo and Santeria for their various purposes.

Elegua (Papa Legba in Voodoo) is used for removing obstacles, and opening opportunities. He also allows for communication with the other spirits. He is called upon first in every ritual to open the doors to the spirit world.

Ogun is the great warrior and is used often for protection. Oshun (Erzuli Freda in Voodoo) is used in love and prosperity rituals. She represents all things beautiful and unconditional love. Yemaya (La Siren in Voodoo) is the great mother who resides in the Ocean. She protects and heals. She especially looks over mothers and their children. Oya is the spirit of the wind, and oversees the world of the dead. She governs change and transition.

Chango is a fierce warrior who represents fire, thunder, and power. He is often sought for bringing justice. Obatala (Damballah in Voodoo) is the wise healer of the pantheon and the closest to God's consciousness. He is sought for wisdom and enlightenment as well as healing.

In both Voodoo and Santeria, there is the religion, and then the magic. One can practice the religion, worshipping God and the spirits, and never engage in spell casting. Some never practice the religion but dabble in the magic. This is where many people of more traditional spiritual paths get confused. There are those who claim to be practitioners of the magical aspects of these ancient traditions but are not following that religious path. There are always those who are looking for the "magic bean," misusing spells and rituals intended for other more benign purposes. Usually when someone uses the magic inappropriately, it is discovered that the person had little knowledge of the true religion. True followers of these religions walk the path dedicated to spirit with the intent of spiritual evolution.

It is never a religion at fault but human nature when violent crimes occur. The criminal mind looks for anyone other than himself for the inability to conform to the rules of society. Often, these people believe to be the victim themselves. It's always someone else's fault that they behave the way they do; their parents, society, and even a religion.

Sometimes mental illness is to blame. Son of Sam murderer, David Berkowitz, heard "voices of demons" that instructed him to kill. The demons were actually the symptoms of mental illness. In schizophrenia, patients often hear voices that they sometimes attribute to someone other than themselves. They disassociate from their own inner dialogue. Many a killer has believed that the voices he heard in his head were those of some deity calling him to a higher level of existence.

Miami has its own occult crime division to handle ritualistic or occult based crime. Occult crimes like all others, vary in degree and severity. In 1986, police broke up a fight between two women who were neighbors. One of them had left a fetish (charm) on the doorstep of the other in an attempt to curse her. The fight was broken up and each of them suffered nothing more than a few scratches.

In 1997, police found a beheaded corpse in Evergreen Cemetery, a local potter's field. The corpse had been dug up, its head removed, then propped up against the broken tomb. It was recently burned and covered in plastic. Surrounding the scene were dead chickens, cigars, feathers, and flowers. Police assumed that the corpse was used in some sort of ritual. While one cannot rule out some cult activity being present, more than likely the perpetrator was not the one who left the offerings. It is highly likely that someone broke into the tomb, desecrated the corpse, and left it. The offerings might well have been left by others, seeing the dead disrespected, made an attempt to give offerings to the spirit to make up for the act of violence.

In the case of Hulon Mitchell, Jr. he practiced neither Voodoo nor Santeria. He was the son of a Christian Pentecostal preacher from Oklahoma. He grew up to become the self-proclaimed "Black Messiah" and leader of infamous Yahweh ben Yahweh cult. Long before he emerged as the leader of this violent cult, his childhood was marred with extreme mood swings, including crying fits and hysterical laughter. Clearly his descent from a strict Christian upbringing to extreme cult activity was a result of his mental illness.

Mitchell became enamored with the Black Muslim movement and Malcolm X in the 1960s. He moved to Atlanta to pursue an education and follow a new religion. Calling himself Mitchell X he began conducting his own services following his leader in promoting black supremacy. Fearing for his life after Malcolm X's assassination, he went into hiding later emerging as a different religious leader. As Father Mitchell, he created his own church calling it the "Modern Christian Church." Now he could make his own rules, and live by his own creed. But by the mid-1070s his church had disbanded leaving Mitchell once again weary for change. He left Atlanta and reinvented himself once again, this time in Orlando, Florida.

In Orlando, Mitchell portrayed himself as a street preacher, calling himself "Brother Love." He pursued studies now in Judaism becoming convinced that the true Jews were black. He relocated to Miami in 1978 starting a church he called "Black Hebrew Israelites" or "Yahwehs." His cult Yahweh ben Yahweh was born.

Mitchell appealed to the poor and the broken in the ghettos of Miami. He urged his followers to kill "white devils" and bring back body parts as proof of the killings. Killing wasn't all the Mitchell did. He used his religion to prey upon young girls, molesting and raping in the name of God. He terrorized Miami for over a decade with his hatred of whites.

On Friday, November 13, 1981 the headless body of twenty-five-year-old Ashton Green was found discarded in the Everglades. Mitchell's followers beheaded Green at Mitchell's instruction for leaving the cult. The cult followers went to kill many others at Mitchell's will. The police were never able to prove that Mitchell actually murdered anyone but did have him arrested and convicted on conspiracy charges. Mitchell spent ten years in prison and was released in August, 2001. He and his followers moved the cult to Canada shortly thereafter. Mitchell died in 2007 of prostate cancer.

Francisco del Junco began seeing a psychiatrist at age 7 after he fell from a third-floor window suffering a head injury. After the fall, he suffered from seizures his entire childhood. In his teens he first started seeing visions and hearing voices. He claimed to see black Santeros, priests of Santeria, who threatened him with evil spells and told him to kill.

In 1993, he was diagnosed as a paranoid schizophrenic and put on medication, which he rarely took. His crime spree began mainly with burglaries. He told doctors of his spiritual visions and how he felt the need to kill. He killed four homeless women by bludgeoning them to death. Although he never practiced Santeria, he blamed the religion for the visions and the voices that instructed him to commit the murders. He now sits in the Union Correctional Facility in Raiford, Florida.

A strange twist of fate brought one criminal to justice despite his attempts to protect himself with a religion. On May 22, 1996, the body of James

Thompson, a forty-year-old computer analyst, was found in his home stabbed to death. He had been dead four days.

The first lead was a phone call made from the dead man's phone, after his death. The call was made to a Santerian House of Prayer. The occult squad traced the call to the church. The Santero remembered the call. He went on to report that the caller was looking for a particular medium who could communicate with the dead, Leonardo Aranda.

Police tracked down Aranda's mother and learned that the caller was her son's lover, Rudolfo Ramirez. The couple had an argument shortly before the murder then reunited some time afterward attending a service at the House of Prayer.

Police returned to the House of Prayer and learned that Ramirez had arranged a special spiritual reading. He sought protection from a guardian angel. The Santero told police that he remembered seeing bloody wounds on Ramirez's swollen hands. He also stated that the reading revealed that Ramirez was guilty of something. He claimed he saw death and violence in the reading. With the Santero's help police eventually were able to obtain evidence convicting Ramirez for the murder

Local Haunts

"When they talk of ghosts of the dead who wander in the night with things still undone in life, they approximate my subjective experience of this life." ~ Jack Henry Abbott

There are a wide variety of haunted locations throughout Miami and surrounding area. Given its volatile history and legacy of murders, it's no wonder. Most hauntings are what parapsychologists call residual hauntings. There might not be an active, intelligent entity present, but merely an energetic impression left from trauma, strong emotions, or even a repetitive action. The lack of a ghost being present in a particular location does not necessarily mean it's less haunted. Residual energy can be extremely strong and have adverse effects on those who are sensitive to psychic energy. The residual haunting is similar to a tape that plays on loop. It can be visual, auditory, or olfactory.

Olfactory residuals tend to be the strongest. One tends to smell something before hearing or seeing it. A good example of this would be a location where a fire had taken place. The smell of smoke can often remain as a residual.

The second most prevalent type of residual would be the auditory. In many haunted locations, residual sounds such as music playing or even conversations can be heard. These types of residual sounds can often be picked up as electronic voice phenomena (EVP). Some people assume if they get EVP, it confirms an intelligent entity present, but sometimes it is only residual. The visual residual is the least common. Usually a scene is played out repeatedly.

The apparitions in the scene are not aware of their surroundings, nor can they communicate. Residual hauntings are not easily documented. They do not appear on photographs, although sometimes the auditory ones will manifest on a digital audio recorder.

One of the most profound residual hauntings could be found at Casa Casuarina. I happened to be visiting Miami for the first time, just weeks after the Versace murder. On my first night in South Beach, I wandered the streets late one evening, taking in the ambiance. As I turned a particular corner, I was hit with a heavy, negative energy that sent a chill up my spine. The feeling was that of sheer terror. I felt impending doom as I walked slowly past the high hedge row then found myself standing directly in front of the doorstep of Casa Casuarina. The gate was chained and locked; the mansion shrouded in darkness. The shock, fear and sadness Versace experienced as he was left bleeding to death mixed with the explosive rage of the killer left a strong impression on the steps. I took several photographs of the front of the home. On a couple of them, a huge orb hovered at the front door. I became so overwhelmed by the energy however, I had to leave the location. This was one haunted experience that I hope I never encounter again, one so recent, and so tragic.

A vast majority of all hauntings are residuals. This explains why it is so difficult to document all phenomena. On television shows, we only see the investigators obtaining actual evidence. What the show fails to reveal is the many hours involved when nothing can be documented. It is difficult for the residual energy to be captured during filming; it's present on a different plane other than the physical. Residual hauntings are very subtle as well. They are usually only noticed when there is no distraction. This explains why some hauntings are only noticed late at night. These subtle energetic changes are noted when there is no other noise or the person experiencing them is in an altered state such as just waking up. Suddenly that which would be ignored at any other time becomes prevalent and more noticeable.

This is why many people have come to believe that haunted phenomena occurs only in the wee hours of the morning when in reality, there is no "bewitching hour." This also explains why many locations can be considered extremely more haunted than others but with less documented evidence. Lack of physical evidence does not prove nor does it disprove anything. Residual hauntings can be extremely strong and are very real even when lacking in physical evidence. Residual hauntings can be present along with intelligent hauntings. The difference between the two is that the intelligent haunting can communicate and is aware of its presence on our plane. Such is the case with many of Miami's haunted places. The Colony Theater began in 1934 as one of the original Paramount Theater chains. The theater was later purchased by Sam Kipnes, a Russian immigrant, who operated it as a movie theater. He bequeathed the theater to the city upon his death. In 1976, Miami spent over a million dollars renovating the old Art Deco theater into a performance art center.

It seems Mr. Kipnes never left the building. The figure of an elderly man wearing a brown suit is often seen sitting alone in the balcony. His footsteps can be heard going up the balcony stairs and walking behind the stage. One security guard, who was alone in the building late one evening, witnessed a man fitting the same description wandering behind stage then disappearing into the curtains. He called the police reporting a break in. When the police arrived, they searched the building completely but found nothing. When they left, the eerie footsteps were heard again behind the curtain. Some believe Kipnes continues to visit the theater because he loved it so much. Or perhaps it's merely his impression, a residual, left from the strong emotional ties he had to the property.

Another famous haunt in Miami is the Jockey Club. In 1907, land developers James Harrison Bright and Glenn Curtiss bought 17,000 acres of swampland on the outskirts of the Everglades. The area frequently flooded and was of little use to anyone. The two men had the swamp basin drained and began development. Some of the land was donated as churches, schools, and municipalities. The rest set aside to sell as middle class subdivisions. The city of Hialeah was incorporated in 1921. In an effort to attract home buyers, they decided to build a horse track. The Jockey Club was built in 1925.

Unfortunately, however, horse betting was illegal in Florida until 1931. The club operated illegally until the Supreme Court ordered a ban on betting at the club in 1927. The owners, determined to make money on their venture, found a way around the ban. They sold what they called "buying options." Betters were sold stock certificates, in the form of post cards. The winners received a stock dividend, the losers found themselves bankrupt.

Once betting became legalized, the club was purchased by Joseph Widener and continued to race horses until 2001. Since its closing, the Jockey Club has sat vacant. The only life that remains is a skeleton crew to maintain it and a small flock of flamingos that still call the park home. Occasionally the property is rented out for a large party or wedding. The ghostly sounds of the club's heyday still echo throughout the club. One security guard heard men arguing and a fight break out in the parking garage late one evening. But when he entered the garage, he heard nothing but silence. No one was there.

In nearby Hialeah Miami Lakes Senior High School resides the ghost of a young man known only as Fred. No one has ever seen Fred but it seems he gets blamed when things go wrong around the school. Tim Flay, a drama teacher, gave an interview to the

Miami Herald in 2005 telling of some of his experiences with Fred. He claimed that most of Fred's activities are limited to the auditorium and a classroom referred to as the "Little Theater."

Flay described to the Herald that each night he shuts down the lights and computers in his classroom. In the morning, he returns to find all of the computers turned on. The activity became so frequent that he started to leave the computers on at night. He also described objects being moved around the classroom. Flay stated, "You look everywhere for something, then return to where it should have been and there it is."

Fred's favorite object is a device called a clap box. It's a theater prop that makes a clapping sound. Often the box sounds off with no one prompting it. Other Miami schools claim to have their own resident ghosts. A young couple haunts the auditorium at the South Dade High School. Stage and flood lights come on late at night. The silhouette of a couple sometimes appears on the stage and the faint sound of music plays. There are also reports of books being rearranged in the library when the school is closed. A female student at Miami Senior High reported seeing a girl, covered in blood, in the girls' bathroom. The figure walked towards her then turned revealing a knife stuck in her back. Before she could scream, the figure vanished.

Julia Morton, a local botanist and author, had lost her home in 1992 during Hurricane Andrew. She moved into the University of Miami's Media Relations building where she worked. Ms. Morton published several books on plants but became famous for her work with poisonous plants. She was an expert consultant to the Poison Control Center. She taught at the University for over four decades. On August 28, 1996, she was critically injured in an automobile accident, never to recover. She died September 10.

Students continue to see the ghost of Julia Morton wandering in the building. She is distinguished by a particular headdress she wore during her life. She's usually seen walking from her office across the courtyard, up the stairwell, then vanishing. Her life and her love was her work at the University. It is there where she remains.

Every city has its own version of popular urban legends. Miami's most frequent urban legend ghost is that of a young girl who attended LaSalle High School. In a field adjacent to the school and Mercy Hospital, she appears walking the field and disappearing into the night. Some accounts say that she committed suicide over a lost love, and others claim that she died from an accidental overdose on the field. Some accounts portray her in seventies attire, others say she died in the eighties. Although she usually appears at night, some have claimed to see her during the day, mistaking her for a game participant on the field. When approached by curious students or security guards, she vanishes. It is uncertain as to the exact date of her death or the cause. Regardless of the details of who she is and how she died, her ghost is real. She remains a mystery and continues to make her ethereal appearances to this day on the vacant, dark field late at night.

Haunted Hotels

"The stones themselves are thick with history, and those cats that dash through the alleyways must surely be the ghosts of the famous dead in feline disguise." ~ Erica Jong

Schools and theaters are not the only haunted buildings in Miami. Many of the local hotels have ghostly residents dwelling within. The Redland Hotel and Historic Inn is situated in Homestead, on the edge of the Everglades. It's a quaint little hotel offering modest accommodations.

The original hotel was built in 1904. It was the first commercial building and hotel in Homestead. It sat directly across from the railroad depot and its initial intent was to serve as a store and boarding house. The structure burned down in 1913 and a new hotel built in its place.

Employees call room 203 "the forgotten room." During the 100th year renovation of the inn, strange manifestations took place. Tearing into walls and floors sometimes awaken hauntings long settled. Once renovations began, objects moved about the room and others disappeared completely. Reports of a woman outside the building, vanishing into room 203 emerged. Although her identity is unknown, it is believed that she committed suicide in the room sometime in the 1930s. Something happened during that renovation to awaken her spirit. She still haunts the inn today.

Another suicide victim is believed to haunt the Miami River Inn. This ghost, however, is a bit more active than the one in Homestead. The inn is located in the oldest part of Miami and situated on the edge of Miami River. Henry Flagler and various U.S. presidents have stayed there during their visits. Guests and inn staff report seeing a mysterious woman in white in the Flagler and Tuttle cabins. Again, details are sketchy as to who she is or when she died there. No one knows why she took her own life on the property, yet they know she is there. The epicenter of activity is in the first front room and occurs regularly at 11:00 PM.

Visitors experience the sound of the front door opening then slamming shut. It's followed by the sound of feet wiping on the doormat, then footsteps running toward the room. Suddenly, the doorknob shakes violently as if someone is desperately trying to enter the room. Many reported actually seeing the doorknob turning then the sound of glass breaking outside followed by a brief silence. The sounds of running feet are heard going up the stairs. For the better part of the next hour noises similar to furniture moving are heard from above. This scene is reenacted over and over again each night.

Perhaps the death wasn't a suicide at all but a murder. A frantic victim tries desperately to find safe haven in the room, only to be found by her attacker and dragged up the stairs reliving the gruesome murder that was never acknowledged. Her body was probably found, dismissed as a suicide and forgotten. Every night she attempts to find safety inside the inn only to meet her violent demise again (and again.)

The Intercontinental Hotel staff tells of an eerie tale based on local superstition. The rocks that were used to build the hotel were supposed to have been strategically arranged in the exact order in which they were quarried. During construction, they were somehow put in the wrong order, altering the harmony of the striations.

The architect, upon learning of the error, flung himself from the rooftop, plummeting to his death. Doorknobs turn, lights and appliances go on, and footsteps are heard throughout the hotel. On certain nights his deadly descent is seen as his body falls from the rooftop, and his final screams echoes into the night.

The most famous of haunted hotels in Miami is the Biltmore Hilton located in the lavish suburban Coral Gables area. The "Beautiful City," as it is so rightly called is a cultural Mecca. It is home to twenty-two parks, thirty-three tennis courts, seven theaters, museums, thirty-eight art galleries, and the largest botanical garden in the continental U.S., the Fairchild Tropical Gardens.

Vintage trollies ride down oak-lined streets through the historical shopping district. One of the most magnificent wonders of Coral Gables is the Venetian Pool, built in 1923. What began as an ordinary rock quarry was transformed into the world's most beautiful swimming pool. The 820,000 gallon, spring-fed pool contains a couple of waterfalls and caves to add to its majesty.

George Merrick built the Biltmore Hilton in 1926 as one of the most fabulous hotels in all of the area. Adorned in copper, its ninety-three-foot tower was modeled after the Giralda bell tower at the Seville Cathedral in Spain. This exclusive resort hotel has catered to both European and Hollywood royalty. The Duke and Duchess of Windsor were guests at the hotel as were famous stars such as Ginger Rogers, Judy Garland, and Bing Crosby. Al Capone ran a speakeasy out of his elaborate suite.

The famous swimming pool at the Biltmore hosted a variety of aquatic shows for its guests. Hollywood's first Tarzan, Johnny Weissmuller, began his career at the pool as a swimming instructor. He later broke the world record for swimming at the Biltmore.

During World War II, the hotel served as a hospital. During that time, some of the windows were sealed with concrete and the marble floors covered in linoleum. It was the early location of the University of Miami, School of Medicine and a VA hospital. It remained a hospital facility until 1968. The ballroom used for a vast majority of weddings today was formerly a morgue.

In 1973 the building was given to Coral Gables but remained vacant for a decade. It was then that residents in the area began to notice the ghostly activity. Neighbors heard strange sounds and saw lights coming from the deserted resort. Renovations began in 1983 and lasted for three years. It was during construction that activity increased. Most of the ghosts are soldiers from the hospital days. An unknown spirit of a young girl has been also seen walking on what is a golf course today. A pair of mild mannered ghosts who are often seen in the hotel and walking the grounds are believed to be George Merrick and his wife. The couple strolls about arm in arm, watching over the property.

One day a hotel employee entered an elevator and before she could select her floor, the elevator doors closed rapidly and proceeded to the sixth floor that was unused at the time. The elevator had been disabled from stopping there, yet the doors opened to what was called "The Bridal Floor." Many years before, a young bride was abandoned by her new husband, resulting in her suicide. While the floor was being renovated construction workers claim to have seen a woman wearing a wedding gown float about then fade away.

One engineering supervisor experienced a strange encounter in the Granada Room. As he checked the doors to the mezzanine one evening, he noticed a couple dancing in a circle in one corner. At first he thought they had wandered in to enjoy a romantic moment then suddenly a chill ran down his spine. He realized that something wasn't right with them. A beam of light shining in from a window shone through the figures. They circled into what appeared to be a misty haze then faded into darkness.

On the third floor, the apparition of an unidentified man appears in doorways and walks into a room toward the bed, then gets in. Several female guests have been startled by a man climbing into bed with them who then disappears when they scream.

The seventh floor is home to the ghost of one of Al Capone's bodyguards. One staff member reported that between 1:00 and 2:00 AM the entire floor becomes icy cold. The sounds of doors slamming are heard throughout the floor. A dark, ominous presence is sensed.

The most haunted floor is the thirteenth. Gangster Fats Walsh operated an illicit casino there. And it was there that he was brutally shot to death. Today, that floor is used as a penthouse and accessible only with a key. Sometimes the elevator will automatically go to the 13th floor, its doors open then shut abruptly then descends. Walsh's bloodstains can still be seen appearing in one bathroom of the suite. A hotel guest once remarked while in the elevator that Fats got what he deserved. Suddenly, the elevator came to a stop between floors. Another guest suggested to the man that he apologize to Fats for his comment. When he did, the elevator started up again. Fats Walsh is said to be a mischievous ghost. He enjoys turning lights on and off, slamming doors, and hiding objects. His favorite trick is to tamper with the elevator.

The Biltmore is considered to be the most haunted hotel in Miami. Given its history, it's no wonder.

Haunted Houses

"They say that shadows of deceased ghosts/ Do haunt the houses and the graves about/Of such whose life's lamp went untimely out/Delighting still in their forsaken hosts." ~ Joshua Sylvester

Of all the ghost stories in Miami, the most popular are found in its mansions, as singer Ricky Martin discovered when he purchased the Wolfson Mansion. The 7,700 square foot estate was built in 1937 by the parents of a young woman who was killed on her way to her wedding. When the Wolfson's bought the home, they were warned by the previous owners not to make any changes to house. Ignoring the warnings, the couple decided immediately to change the draperies. As they removed the old drapes, they heard a dreadful moan echo through the house. The spiteful spirit proceeded to tear down ceiling tiles and turned appliances on and off. Mr. Wolfson hired an exorcist on three different occasions to rid the property of what he described as a "vindictive old-maidish sort of figure." Perhaps the ghost of the young bride who never made it to her wedding, continued to resent that her life was cut short, never having fulfilled her dreams.

The Witherspoon House is a modest suburban home haunted by a malevolent ghost. On February 25, 1962, Carrington Harvey Witherspoon was shot and killed by his wife. Witherspoon was an abusive husband and father. He had brutally beaten his thirteen-year-old son with a chair. Mrs. Witherspoon, fearing for her son's life, killed her husband in a desperate attempt to stop the abuse.

At her trial, witnesses testified that Mr. Witherspoon frequently abused his wife and children. He not only beat them but broke furniture over their injured bodies and shot his shotgun to frighten and control them. The court determined that Mrs. Witherspoon was under extreme duress at the time she committed the murder and she was acquitted. The terror had ended but not the tragedy for Mrs. Witherspoon. Only a few months after the murder, her sixteen-year-old son was killed on a motorcycle right outside the home. The broken woman sold the home and moved what was left of her family.

The new owners became the victims. All hours of the day and night, furniture moved about and loud crashing sounds were heard. They felt an intense uneasiness and often smelled a foul stench. In 1967, they hired a medium to communicate with the disgruntled spirit. The medium claimed to contact the ghost of Carrington Witherspoon and that the angry man vowed to return to get even with his wife for killing him.

Famed aviation pioneer, Glenn Curtiss built his pueblo-style mansion on Deer Run. Often called the father of naval aviation, Curtiss was the co-developer in the city of Hialeah. The estate covered over thirty acres and included a lake complete with swans and flamingos, and a tennis court.

Today, the house sits vacant on an overgrown lot awaiting renovation. Passersby, see lights flickering inside. Screams are heard coming from within. Some claim to see ghostly tennis players on the court late at night. But no one seems to know the real story behind the hauntings.

One version of the story claims that Glenn Curtiss went mad after discovering his wife had an abortion. In this version, he punished her brutally with abuse then ignored her. In an act of revenge for his wrath, Mrs. Curtiss burned the house down with him inside. Others claim that he did indeed go mad, but it was he who burned down the house with his wife and children inside.

The latest research proves that whether Mrs. Curtiss had an abortion or not, she and her husband lived in the property together until his death in 1930 due to complications of appendicitis surgery. She then remarried a business associate of her late husband and they resided in the home for another ten years. The house was burned apparently by vandals sometime after that; but what about the ghosts?

The house is still vacant and people still report hearing sounds and seeing apparitions about. Not all hauntings are caused from some terrible murder. Perhaps there was no murder. Perhaps just another residual haunting left over from those who lived there who merely loved the home. Their ghosts long gone but the emotional ties still remain. Regardless of whether emotions are positive or negative, they certainly leave an impression on our earth plane. In the case of the Stranahan House, it is misfortune that forged its impression in the now haunted home.

Frank Stranahan was one of the area's first settlers. He built his home along with a trading post and a bank on the New River in Fort Lauderdale, twenty-six miles north of Miami. Stranahan founded Fort Lauderdale and is responsible for the first ferry that crossed the river allowing for easy travel toand from Miami. Sadly, he eventually wound up broke and developed cancer. Severe depression set in which led to his suicide on the property. He tied a portion of metal fence to his leg, and plunged to his death in the river. His ghost has been seen reenacting the suicide on the edge of the river. Some claim to see his spirit darting into the highway that now cuts through what was once his property.

One of the employees of the Stanahan House Museum reported seeing an impression in one of the beds as if someone was seated there. She said she smelled perfume that she believes to be that of Stranahan's wife, Ivy. She keeps records of ghostly activity in the house and estimates it to occur at least four times a month. Photographs document bright orbs and ectoplasm as well.

The most famous haunted house in Miami is Villa Paula. The neoclassical mansion was built in 1925 as the Cuban Consulate. It has ten rooms, two baths, eighteen-foot ceilings, and hand-painted floor tiles. The Villa was built with yellow bricks that were imported from Cuba, covered in white stucco.

The first Cuban Consul, Domingo Milford and his beautiful wife, Paula, occupied the home. There is very little documented about Paula's life. What is known is that she died from complications after a leg amputation, only six years after moving into the home. It can be assumed that Paula died amidst strong emotions of pain and sorrow. She was still quite young and active when she tragically lost her leg in an accident. Still very traumatized from the loss, she died unexpectedly from shock shortly after the surgery. Her sad, restless spirit still resides in the property.

The next to own the Villa was Muriel Reardon who owned the home for thirty years. Later, the house became a home for the elderly. No doubt other deaths have occurred there over the years. The house eventually fell into ruins and became a haven for drifters. It was 1974 when antique dealer Cliff Ensor purchased and refurbished the house.

Numerous magazines and newspapers over the 1970s and 1980s interviewed Ensor. When the house was sold, an article appeared in the Miami Herald stating, "Buyer Beware." The Herald listed the sale as "For Sale: Historic Villa Paula in Little Haiti. Needs some work; an exorcism couldn't hurt." Although Paula is blamed for most of the activity, its undetermined which ghosts are the most active.

The smell of Cuban coffee is often noticed. Other times, the sounds of a piano playing can be heard. Doors slam and footsteps heard running down the hall. One ghost threw a temper tantrum in the kitchen, throwing dishes and silverware about. On another occasion, the front porch chandelier suddenly came loose from its socket and crashed to the floor.

Other reports include the sounds of high heels coming up the stone path followed by a steady tapping on the door.

When Ensor told an elderly neighbor of his bedroom door slamming the neighbor replied, "That's Paula. She always hated to have a draft on her shoulders when she played piano in that room."

It is the same room where Paula's untimely death took place. The ghost of Paula, a tall, olive-skinned woman, is usually seen wearing a black dress with a ruffled neckline and sleeve.

One sad incident involved what is believed to be the ghost of Muriel Reardon and Cliff Ensor's pet cats. Muriel hated cats. Ensor had three cats when he moved into the home. One by one, each of them died while crossing through the iron-gate onto the property. As the animals reached the threshold of the gate, it slammed shut onto them. There was no physical reason to account for these accidents. There was no wind. But on each occasion, as the animal passed through the gate, it slammed shut like a trap. It's believed that Muriel still considers the home her own. She would have never allowed cats to live on the property.

Ensor witnessed two full-bodied apparitions during his stay in the house. One he saw only as a shadow that faded and then disappeared. The other was a tall Cuban woman with black hair pulled tightly into a bun walking down the hallway with only one leg.

In 1976, Ensor brought in a psychic and a spiritualist to conduct a séance. Several people were present as the medium went into a trance and began to speak. She stated that Paula was too shy to speak herself but that she loved Cuban coffee, roses, and music from "Carmen." She saw and channeled several other entities as well, a man who wore a top hat and a woman dressed in red. These are probably ghosts left over from the days of the retirement home. There was one woman who appeared to the medium who was crying for a medal she had lost in the garden. Another woman appeared who searches for the grave of her illegitimate baby who had died before her. The psychic believed her to possibly be a maid who worked at the mansion. The psychic also reported that the ghosts of Paula and Muriel Reardon often fight over the rights of the house. This could account for the dish smashing in the kitchen.

In the late 1980s Ensor sold the house. Today the building is used as a doctor's office. But a local paranormal investigation team recently revealed that a new property claimed the title as the most haunted house in Miami. The 444 acre Deering Estate and Gardens, an environmental, archeological and historical preserve offers tours, art exhibits, concerts, and festivals; and overnight ghost expeditions.

Entrepreneur and art collector, Charles Deering built his mansion on the property in 1900. His wife opened an inn there calling it The Richmond Cottage. In 1920, he built the stone mansion to protect his family and art collection from fires and storms. An avid art collector, Charles Deering collected 4,000 pieces of fine art worth sixty million dollars in 1922.

The ground itself proved to be quite a rare and valuable archaeological gem. Human fossils carbon-dated 10,000 years old were discovered on the property. Animal fossils over 100,000 years old have also been found. In addition to Paleo-Indians, the oldest civilization in North America, there's evidence of a Tequesta village existing there at one time. Down the historic Tequesta Trail lies a burial mound in the hard wood hammock.

Many of the most haunted places in America are built on what was once Native American burial ground. Most experts agree that it is no coincidence. When these people buried their dead in what was to them sacred ground, they did not anticipate later civilizations coming along and building on top of them. In ancient cultures, specific spirits guarded these sacred places. Much of the ghostly activity found in these areas is the guarding spirits still doing their job. Usually, there are no problems when the property and spirits of those buried there are treated with respect. But when ghost enthusiasts disrespect or taunt such spirits, problems can arise.

In addition to the Native spirits residing on the property, a tragic accident occurred in 1916. An explosion killed five Bahamian workers who were dredging the channel on the property.

A local paranormal group claim to have witnessed two full-bodied apparitions on the property. According to a report done by the League of Paranormal Investigators of Coconut Grove, two translucent figures, a male and a female, were photographed in the boat basin of Biscayne Bay, on the edge of the estate. The group also claims to have recorded numerous disembodied voices at the estate. On a different investigation, the misty apparition of a woman dressed in a flowing white dress was seen in the same place.

Strange sounds are heard in both the cottage and the stone house. Doors slam, loud crashes, and ghostly footsteps are frequently reported. Shadowy figures wander in and out of the buildings and all about the property. One of the ghosts present is believed to be that of Charles Deering's brother, James Deering. James frequented the property during his life and shared his brother's love of art. His ghost is also said to haunt his nearby former home, the Vizcaya Museum and Gardens.

Many have claimed to have seen a women dressed in 1920s-era clothing wandering through the gardens. One investigator claimed to have photographed the apparition of a man on the stairs inside the museum. One photograph displayed on the internet clearly showed a misty-like figure of a man surrounded by many orbs. The figure had no distinguishable facial features so it's not a living person. Yet, it has the identifiable form of a man.

The activity at the Deering Estate stirred so much controversy between believers and skeptics when first researched in 2009 that a local businessman publicly offered one million dollars to anyone who could provide "solid, irrefutable evidence of a paranormal event." Presumably the reward has not been paid to anyone. I guess photographic evidence of an ethereal figure isn't proof enough. He never specified what he would consider actual proof. As with most skeptics, he will probably never be convinced. And as with most believers, lack of evidence does not disprove the existence of paranormal phenomena.

For those who want to find their own proof, the Deering Estate now offers special ghost tours of the property and overnight ghost hunting adventures to the public. This is one Miami location that backs up its haunting with a "see for yourself" offer.

Tropical Poltergeist

"Madness is tonic and invigorating. It makes the sane more, sane. The only ones who are unable to profit by it are the insane." ~ Henry Miller.

One of the most misunderstood type of haunting is the poltergeist. It literally means "noisy ghost" in German. Poltergeist activity is defined by loud, unexplained noises and the physical movement of objects. Poltergeist activity can be caused by an intelligent haunting, but that is rare. Most of it is attributed to very strong emotional psychic energy that is often caused by the living.

A large percentage of what is considered poltergeist activity is in reality uncontrolled energy from an adolescent or mentally disturbed individual. Emotions that are not expressed become stored in the body. These repressed emotions can later manifest themselves in the physical body as pain, disease or emotional disturbances. Sometimes however, rather than storing in the body, the emotional energy gets thrown off into the physical plane and can be experienced as what might be perceived as psychic phenomena. This is particularly true in instances where an individual is more psychically sensitive.

To the untrained individual, it would be a normal reaction to assume that this type of energy disbursement would be coming from an outside source. When in reality, the energy is coming from an internal source. A good example of this type of energy disbursement can be explained best in the case of repressed anger. Anger is a particularly volatile emotion. If the anger is not expressed, it turns inward. In individuals who have mastered not being in touch with their emotions or denying them, the anger gets buried deep in the physical body. Many years later, pain and illness manifest caused by the stored emotions. For those individuals who have a hard time controlling their emotions and because of guilt or other stress attempt to push it inward, this anger could very well project itself externally resulting in physical pain or disease.

For individuals who struggle to contain intense emotions, they may have a tendency to project that excess energy through psychic means. If you have ever encountered a person who was angry or upset over something and trying to conceal that emotion, you know exactly the type of energy field that is surrounding such a person. Even though the person is smiling and saying there is nothing wrong, they carry an aura that clearly indicates that there is an underlying problem. One can "feel" the negative energy projecting from the individual despite the attempt to conceal it.

Another example is in dealing with those who are mentally or emotionally ill. There is a certain energy that surrounds such individuals that gives a feeling of "something not right" to those around them. Depressed people are often described as having a "black cloud over them." Manic people have a fast paced or racing type of energy around them. This is why moods can be contagious. It is the energy from particular individuals and how others receive it. Enthusiastic people send out enthusiastic vibrations that can be felt by others, who in turn begin to feel enthusiastic. Negative people send out negative vibrations that can bring others down or make them feel tired. It is all part of the normal human energetic field.

In adolescents, the energy changes and matures rapidly due to hormonal surges. Just as the adolescent has to adjust to the physical changes in the body, energetic changes must also be taken into consideration. Changes in the body occur in the energetic level first. This is true of everything in the universe. This is why one of the principals of magic is "as above, so below."

Magic is the manipulation of thought, desires, and beliefs and manifesting change on the physical level. The changes occur on the energetic level, as above; then slowly manifest on the physical level, so below. Long before the child begins to experience the bodily changes of adolescence, the energetic changes have begun. The child is unaware of these subtle energetic changes. The energy surges as do later the hormones, thus resulting in projections of excess energy. This is a time of irrational emotions, again caused by hormonal surges within the body. Just as the child is unaware of why his or her emotions are in an uproar, the same holds true for the energetic field. The energy sometimes is projected out of the body and creates movement or disruption in and around the child's area. If the energy is being "thrown off" in great amounts, it can cause objects to move about, a kind of involuntary telekinesis if you will.

In an experiment in psychic energy done in a paranormal study class at University of New Orleans, I asked my students to form a circle connecting hands at the palms. Each student had one palm up, and the other down. This is done to prevent an obstruction of energy that would occur if the hands were clasped together. The energy moving throughout the circle could be felt as if a current of electricity was pulsing around the circle. They were then asked to concentrate on nothing but the movement of that energy and making it stronger and faster. After five minutes of moving this current of energy, I noticed the clock on the wall. The hands of the clock began to rapidly spin. When I pointed this out to the students, the first impression by most of them was that a "ghost" had come into the room and was moving the clock. When in fact it was the energy created from the circle. When the circle was broken, the clock began to move at a normal pace.

Similar tests were conducted when I was student; using nothing more than two glasses of tap water. Each of us was asked to taste each glass of water. The water of course, tasted the same in both glasses. We were then asked to place our hands around one of the glasses and send positive energy into the water in that glass. We were told to concentrate on feelings of love and well-being while "charging" the water. After several minutes, we were asked to taste the two glasses of water. The water that had been "blessed" with positive energy tasted different from the regular tap water. The energy sent changed the molecular structure of the ordinary tap water, giving it a sweeter taste.

Some parapsychologists believe that poltergeist activity may also be a type of manifestation of an apparition caused by the living projecting an aspect of their own personality.

In December 1966, strange things began to manifest in the Tropical Arts wholesale novelty warehouse. It began with the discovery of some broken glass steins. Soon other merchandise was rolling off of shelves spontaneously and breaking. Within a month, the staff had become so distraught from the disturbances, the management decided to call the police. Patrolman William Killiam was the first to arrive on the scene. Within an hour, he had witnessed so much strange phenomena he called for back-up. The police found no sign of an intruder or break-in.

That's when the owner of the Tropical Arts decided to contact the American Society for Psychical Research. On January 21, 1967 they began a study of the building. In ten days, they validated over 150 manifestations of psychic phenomena. The epicenter of the activity seemed to be a young Cuban employee, nineteen-year-old Julio Vasquez.

Vazquez had a large amount of emotional pressures and stress in his life. The team began to believe that his emotions were disbursing as phenomena in the warehouse. On January 30, Vasquez broke into the warehouse and stole a small amount of petty cash. He was fired but no charges were filed. As soon as Vasquez no longer worked on the premises, all paranormal activity ceased. The team determined that Vasquez had an abnormal amount of psychic energy and was the cause of the disturbances.

Soon thereafter Vasquez was arrested for robbing a jewelry store and went to prison. After his release, he married and had a baby girl. He allowed ASPR to conduct psychic tests on him determining that he had a high ability to produce psychokinetic effects. The Psychic Research Center offered Vasquez a large amount of money to participate in testing for his abilities. Despite living below poverty level with a family to support, he declined the offer. He didn't want to be used as a guinea pig.

Ghosts of The Glades

"Christmas makes everything twice as sad." ~ Doug Coupland

The thick saw grass and dense forests of the Florida Everglades make the location a perfect dumping spot for dead bodies. Well, almost perfect. Countless stories of bodies being found with little or no explanation fill the archives of the Miami Herald. In the late 1970s the body of a well-dressed, middle aged woman was discovered in a canal in the Everglades. Her head had been ripped off by a hungry crocodile or alligator. But the clues to her identity or how she wound up there led investigators nowhere.

In the early morning of March 21, 1999, a local man fishing with his young son noticed a taped up package bobbing along the shoreline. He immediately felt uneasy but decided to reel it and see what was inside. As he walked toward the package, another fisherman warned him to stay away. Curiosity got the best of him and pulled the package closer to him. When he attempted to lift it to determine how heavy it was, the cardboard fell apart and long, brown hair fell out. He tugged a little more and the decomposing corpse of a young woman fell out into the water. Her wrists were tied behind her back and her ankles bound together by shoelaces.

The body was that of a twenty-two-year-old stripper who worked at a local club.

The young woman was identified and as it turned out, her killer was caught. She is one of the unusual cases as most bodies found in the Everglades remain mysteries.

Late at night in the glades, ghostly screams and cries are heard; lights appear then disappear. Sometimes the sound of a plane plunging into the swamp can be heard. Over and over again, the ghost plane of Flight 401 makes its deadly descent into the murky water.

On Friday, December 29th, 1972, Eastern Airlines flight 401 departed from JFK Airport in New York bound for Miami. The jet was a new Lockheed L-1011 Tristar. It stood as high as a five story building and built to carry over two hundred people. The aircraft was under the control of fifty-five-year-old Captain Robert Loft. Loft had twenty-five years of experience working for Eastern Airlines. His engineer and second officer was fifty-one-year-old Donald Repo, another Eastern Airlines veteran of twenty-five years. There were one hundred and seventy six passengers on board that night. Among them was businessman, Jerry Eskew who was to meet his wife in Miami to celebrate New Year's Eve. He and his wife always travelled separately in the event of an accident so she was on another flight. Evelyn de Salazaar, an art gallery manager in Manhattan, traveled alone with her small poodle in a pet carrier under her seat. Gustavo Casado was traveling with his wife, Xiomara, and their two month old daughter, Christina.

Lilly Infantino was traveling with her new husband Ronald to spend the holiday with family in Little Havana. The couple wed on December 10 and were returning from a visit with Ronald's family in New York after their honeymoon. During the flight, Lilly left her window seat to go to the bathroom. Upon her return, Ronald had switched seats with her. The move did not seem consequential at the time but would later prove to save her life.

Twenty-four-year-old Jerrold Solomon was on his way to visit his girlfriend for the holidays. His mother had recently returned from a trip to Israel bringing back a gold Star of David which Jerrold was wearing on a chain around his neck. Newly engaged Jerry Ulrich and Sandra Burt were seated alone in first class. Jerry had just proposed during the flight.

One of Flight 401's regular flight attendants was not on the flight. She called in sick that day but not sick from an illness. She was sick with impending doom. She had been plagued with prophetic nightmares of a plane crash. In her dreams she saw a crashing plane and holly wreaths indicating that the crash would occur close to Christmas. She knew what type of plane it would be and that it would be on a flight to Miami. When offered to fly on flight 401 on that day, she declined fearing the dream might be real. She went home hoping that she'd awaken to find that her nightmares were just bad dreams. Later she would be horrified to learn that Flight 401 disappeared into the Everglades.

As Flight 401 approached Miami, directly ahead was National Airlines Flight 607 which was having difficulty with landing gear. At 11:19 PM Flight 607 was instructed to land. It was at this point that its captain alerted air traffickers that there was a problem with the jet and it would need extra clearing and a fire truck upon landing. Flight 401 was assigned another parallel runway.

As Captain Loft prepared for a landing, he noticed that nose gear indicator light was not working. Loft lifted the aircraft and notified control that he had to circle and wait for the light to come on. It never did. At 11:35 PM, Loft turned the plane over to his co-pilot as he and Repo worked on the light.

Controllers were more concerned with flight 607 which appeared to have a real emergency. The men continued to repair the light which had recently been replaced. Somehow, however, the tiny fixture had been turned sideways. As repairs to the light continued the autopilot yoke accidently got turned off. The out of control jet plunged into the darkness of the swamps, a mere 18.7 miles from the runway. One hundred and one people were killed. Miraculously, seventy-five survived.

At 11:42 PM, a private plane had taken off and called in a report of huge fire in the Everglades. Around that same time, two men who were frog gigging in the area witnessed the ball of fire darting towards the wreckage. By 11:45 PM, Coast Guard helicopters were in search of survivors. The following day, survivors told their story to the media.

The experience was described by several people as a deadly roller coaster ride. Flight attendant, Beverly Raposa described feeling the plane roll to the left. She stated, "I could see my arms going in front of me from side to side and felt my feet also going from side to side. My body was held in tightly by the shoulder harness. But the rest of me was moving along with this jolting."

She saw a ball of flames in the cabin. She went on, "I could see things flying all about me…there was a rush of wind that sounded like we were in the middle of a tornado. The coat closet disappeared. Nothing was there but open space."

Her experience was particularly odd. Three months before the flight, she had visited a psychic who predicted that she would be in a plane crash and would live. The psychic, a Catholic, instructed her to get a medal of Our Lady of Mount Carmel. She wore the medal the night of the crash.

Jerry Solomon remembered seeing a flash of light coming out of the cockpit and hearing the sounds of people crying. After the crash he assisted Beverly Raposa rescuing survivors who were strapped into their seats. All the while Raposa sang Christmas carols to keep spirits up. Airboat captain, Robert Marquis, was the first to arrive on the scene. Almost immediately stories of ghosts of Flight 401 began to surface. John G. Fuller wrote the best-selling book, *The Ghosts of Flight 401*, which later became a movie.

In 1974, a US Flight Safety Foundation's newsletter told of ghostly activity. Sadie Messina waited for husband to arrive on that evening. She told the Miami Herald, "He always had a distinctive little whistle, a code whistle. When I heard this whistle I knew he was home. We were waiting at the gate, my two sons and I heard his whistle. It sounded like he was right behind me. I turned around to look, but of course, he wasn't there." Sadie heard the whistle at the precise time of the crash. Her husband, Rosario Messina, was among the dead.

A female passenger on a later flight found herself sitting next to an Eastern Airlines officer who appeared pale and stoic. The man said nothing, just stared blankly. By the time she could get a flight attendant to come over, the man had vanished. The woman later identified Repo in a photograph.

Repo also appeared to an engineer as he carried out routine flight inspections. Repo told him, "You don't have to worry about the pre-flight, I've already done it."

Again and again, Repo appeared in various areas on different flights that had recycled salvage parts from Flight 401. He was seen by several engineers, one of whom came face to face with him after hearing knocking sounds in the compartment below the cockpit. One captain recalled seeing the ghost of Repo. Repo said to him, "There will never be another crash. We will not let it happen."

A flight attendant, Faye Merryweather, saw Repo's face in the oven of a TriStar 318. She called over two colleagues who not only witnessed the apparition but also heard his voice warn of a fire. The plane later developed engine trouble and was pulled from its flight. The galley of the aircraft had also been built from salvage from Flight 401.

Captain Bob Loft had also been reported on various Eastern flights. A vice president of the airlines once spoke to a uniformed captain seated in first class. He suddenly realized that it was the late Bob Loft, at which point, the apparition disappeared. On another flight, a captain and two attendants spoke with Captain Loft then watched him vanish. They were so upset by the incident that the flight was cancelled.

Flight 401 is not the only plane to have crashed in the Everglades. Numerous small planes and helicopters have plunged into the swamp killing those on board. In May 1996, Valu-Jet Flight 592 carrying 109 passengers plummeted to its demise killing all onboard. Unlike Flight 401, no remains of the plane or passengers were ever found. Flight 592 disappeared shortly after take-off, never to be seen again. Blood-soaked apparitions have been reported being seen walking aimlessly down nearby roads. Cries and moans are still heard echoing in the vacant darkness in the swamp. Ghostly faces often appear beneath the water only to sink down into the black water. The shock and terror that these people experienced in their final moments have left a heavy residual impression on the Everglades. But disembodied cries and ghostly images are not the only frightening things in the swamp. Strange creatures are said to inhabit its dark corners.

Strange Creatures

"Imagination creates some big monsters." ~ Olivier Martinez

No book on unsolved mysteries and paranormal phenomena would be complete without addressing the local cryptids. There are more strange and unexplainable creatures in the Everglades than in most areas. Yet despite countless eyewitness accounts of sightings and encounters, the question still remains, do these strange creatures exist?

Just about anywhere you go you'll find legends of a bigfoot creature. The Florida Everglades is no exception. The Florida version of the creature is called the Florida Skunk Ape. Bigfoot by any other name is still bigfoot so it really doesn't matter what you call it. Color varies depending on the location. Some are gray; others brown, but most have basically the same characteristics. The hairy monster is usually described as being about seven feet tall, having a flat face, broad shoulders, is covered in fur, and has a foul stench.

Accounts of Skunk Ape sightings have cropped up all over Florida. Due to the vastness of the open wilderness of the Everglades, many stories originate there. One witness reported seeing one of the elusive monsters walking along a road in the swamps. She described it as having white around its eyes and a leathery mouth. The creature has been spotted by tour groups, fishermen, and a local fire chief claimed to see the ape walking around his yard then disappearing into the nearby woods. In the 1970s rumors ran rampant of a skunk ape being captured by the military and contained in a secret vault. As the story goes, the mighty animal broke its containment and escaped. Throughout the 1970s numerous sightings were made in various suburban neighborhoods in Dade County.

A truck driver claimed to have hit one on Alligator Alley one night but as with the captive one, it too ran off into the darkness. In 1967, a fisherman claimed to see one coming up from the ocean near the port of Miami. He described an ape-like creature that stood upright about seven tall and weighed about four hundred pounds. Some reports claim the creatures live and breed in caverns near the Miami River.

Footprints have been documented, samples of fur, and droppings found but nothing ever surfaces that gives concrete evidence that the creature actually exists. No one has ever captured one, found a carcass, or even skeletal remains of one. One expert suggested that the animals might cover their dead with leaves and debris or even bury them. I question how there could be so many eye witness accounts from all over the world and never any real proof? Certainly if there were some sort of ape-like creature living in the woodlands of North America, at some point in time, a carcass or skeletal remains would have surfaced. Despite the lack of proof, the sightings continue to spring up not only in the Everglades but in various parts of the country. Perhaps the truth will never surface.

In most cases, logical explanations eventually become evident that explain what was once unexplained. Take the case of the Chupacabra. For years, people reported sightings of the infamous goat sucker who preyed on livestock. It was described as having no hair, a long snout, and short front legs. In 2008, police footage surfaced on the internet showing one of the animals running from a police car on a desert road. Then the truth was revealed when a carcass was found. The elusive Chupacabra turned out to be a coyote with a particular type of mange that causes the hair to fall out, the skin to become a bluish color, and the animal becomes deranged. Because it's sick, it can no longer hunt normally and tends to gravitate to populated areas feeding on livestock.

There seems to be much better documentation when it comes to the sea monsters. The most noted sea monster is Nessy, the Loch Ness monster of Scotland. In 1908, a couple visiting the Miami area claimed to have witnessed a sea monster in the Biscayne Bay. They described a thirty foot creature with a long, slender neck. The story became so controversial that a well-known fisherman, Captain Charles Thomson offered to capture the sea monster. In an article in the Miami Metropolis on July 28, 1908, he told a reporter, "If there is anything that swims of extraordinary dimensions playing peek-a-boo with Captain Charley up around Little River, within a few days, its name will be mud." Needless to say, Thompson never captured the creature.

More recently, the History Channel aired an episode on Monsterquest about a creature spotted in the same vicinity that was captured on film. The huge beast's head was sticking out of the water and behind waved a trident tail. One expert deemed the animal's face indicated that it was a member of the seal family while another disputed that it was a mutilated manatee. A follow up video on YouTube suggested that the animal in question was actually a leopard seal.

The animal in the video fit the description of the leopard seal except for one thing - Leopard seals are not native to South Florida. They are common to the South Atlantic Ocean, the closest to Florida being the coast of South America. I contacted Allan Gilbreath, an expert on unidentified animals and a wealth of crypto-zoological information. If anybody could explain how a leopard seal could wind up in South Florida, it would be Allan. I wrote him a quick email along with a link to the video.

Allan responded, "I love researching cryptids! If you are looking in Florida for weird stuff, you are going to find it wholesale. After about one hundred years of people importing exotic animals and losing them down there, that place could have literally anything in it."

Florida does have quite a few aquatic parks and it is feasible that an imported seal could have somehow gotten loose and made its way into the river. Still, the legend of the elusive Skunk Ape lives on. The creature remains a mystery until someone can come up with solid evidence of its existence.

Allan Gilbreath offered an explanation noting that over time, apes and chimps have escaped from sideshows and jungle movie sets. For many years, some crypto-zoologists have maintained that skunk apes are actually North American apes, or Napes brought over from Africa via slave ships many years ago. The slave trade in Africa began in the 1600s and continued through the 18th century during which time over thirty thousand voyages were made to North America. It is believed that these ships carried more than human cargo.

Napes are very similar to ordinary chimpanzees except that the North American variety can swim; African chimps do not. Maybe they adapted, evolved in a swamp environment. Some researchers believe that they are simply a different variety of chimpanzee.

In his book, *The Apes*, British primatologist, Vernon Reynolds noted the behavior of chimpanzees in Spanish Guineau on the Western African coast, "A report from Spanish Guinea states that four chimpanzees were observed swimming across the 60 to 65-meter-wide Benito River. They made swimming motions like dogs…I am inclined to think that the "chimpanzees" seen swimming in the above report were some other species. The general response of chimpanzees is universally agreed to be one of avoidance and even fear.

I have myself on two occasions helped to pull chimpanzees out of a water-filled moat in which they were quite clearly drowning, and I am convinced they cannot swim."

The idea of a breed of ape having been transported to the New World certainly offers a legitimate explanation of the many sightings of what most people call the skunk ape. Add to that the population of possible apes that may have escaped captivity wandering into the wilds and there could very well be colonies of wild primates living in the Everglades.

Real Monsters of the Everglades

"We create monsters and then we can't control them." ~ Joel Coen

The story is always the same. A large head emerges from the deep. Several feet behind it, a portion of its serpent-like body rises up revealing its scaly back. Someone sees it. Suddenly everyone is talking about the monster in the lake or river. Some say it's a giant fish, others an aquatic dinosaur believed to have been extinct for eons. Curious thrill seekers bring their cameras in hopes of catching proof of existence for some zoological oddity. Then some expert comes along and identifies the monster and ruins it for everyone.

The Everglades is world renowned for its diverse wildlife. It is home to over three-hundred-fifty different species of birds. In addition to the usual deer, raccoons, foxes, and bears found in swamps and forests, it has a variety of mammals unique to its wetlands. The Florida panther is an endangered species. A subspecies of the cougar, there are less than two hundred panthers living in the wild. Manatees live in the dense mangrove forests of the swamps. These docile marine mammals are also endangered with less than twelve hundred left in existence.

The Everglades has over fifty different varieties of reptiles, many of which are quite dangerous. Most people are familiar with the American Alligator and readily associate the animal with the Everglades. The main road cutting through the swamp is called Alligator Alley. The average length of an adult male alligator is about eleven feet in length. Alligators are dark gray or black, have rounded snouts, and stout bodies. Usually, alligators do not attack humans unless they are provoked or very hungry. Most attacks in Florida are largely due to humans populating the alligators' natural environment. What a lot of people do not realize is that in addition to the alligator, the Everglades is home to caiman and crocodiles.

The caiman is a member of the alligator family, although they are much smaller. Caiman are not native to Florida but many were imported from Central and South America and sold as exotic pets. Consequently, the cute babies grew, and people started setting them free in swamps. As with its American cousin, most caiman are harmless unless cornered. Crocodiles are a bit different.

The American Crocodile is found not only in the rivers and swamps of the Everglades but in coastal marshes. It can live in both salt and fresh water. It's much lighter in color than the alligator and has a slim, pointed snout and streamlined body. Crocs tend to be larger than alligators. The average male is about fourteen feet but can grow as large as twenty feet in length. Unlike the alligator or caiman, crocodiles are quite aggressive. Until recent years, these man-eating lizards ruled the Everglades. But a new monster reptile has recently become the most feared in the vast swamp. They probably account for a large percentage of sea serpent sightings in the area. They are growing in number and threatening the delicate ecosystem of the Everglades.

Some people have a fascination with owning exotic pets. The more exotic, rare, and illegal, the more fascinated they become. But for those who choose giant snakes as their pets, the story usually ends the same for all concerned. Over the past several decades, the importing of Burmese pythons and Anacondas has increased. Even responsible pet owners with the best intentions often have to face the realization that their pet snake will eventually become too large to handle. As with the caiman, most pet pythons or anacondas will wind up set free into the wilderness.

Since 2002, more than three-hundred-fifty Burmese pythons have been captured in the Everglades. Experts believe that there could be as many as one-hundred-thousand living giant snakes roaming free. These animals originate in South Asia and thrive is Florida's warm weather. An adult python can grow to over twenty feet in length and weigh over two hundred pounds. The biggest problem is that these animals are carnivorous. They will eat any creature that doesn't eat them first, even large alligators and crocodiles.

Pythons are constrictors. They kill by wrapping around its prey and crushing and suffocating it with its massive muscles. Once an animal or human is in its powerful grip, there's little chance of escape. Because these invaders have no natural predators, it is impossible to naturally keep the population in check. They breed rapidly. One python can lay as many as a hundred eggs.

In addition to the python invasion, anacondas have also been found inhabiting the Everglades. The green anaconda can grow as long as forty feet. Like the python, they will consume most other animals including other anacondas. With eyes and nostrils located on top of its enormous head, the anaconda can wait completely submerged in water until it strikes. It's a very aggressive snake.

Some scientists believe that because of their rate of breeding, these giant snakes could eventually take over the entire Southeastern part of the U.S. They would become the largest predators on the continent. They would upset the ecosystem, possibly wiping out other native species. The risk to humans would be great. Imagine if such creatures began to breed in other lakes and rivers outside of the Everglades.

The Asian Swamp Eel is a scale-less eel that is found in fresh water in Asia. Somehow this odd looking creature has found its way into the canals, lakes, and marshes of South Florida. In Asia, the eels are commonly farmed for food. In South Florida, it has no natural enemies. It's a predatory carnivore that preys on fish, amphibians, and small reptiles, threatening the natural fauna of South Florida. The average size is about three feet long and weighs about a pound.

This little swamp monster could easily be mistaken for some sort of mutant cryptid or even something from another planet. It survives in either fresh or brackish water. Unlike most eels, which are usually classified as a type of fish, the Asian Swamp Eel can breathe in water and out of water. It can also slither on land like a snake. But the weirdest aspect of the eel is that it is transgender. Many are born female, develop as female then transform into large males. These males guard the nests.

Another Asian invading species is what the media calls the "Frankenfish." The Asian Snakehead is an aggressive fish with canine-like teeth. Like the eel, the Snakehead is farmed for food in Asia. The brave fishermen who farm them in the ponds of Asia wear protective clothing due to the fish's aggressive nature. Like the eel, young fish are sold as pets on the internet and innocent buyers soon find that these "monsters" eat whatever else is in the tank. The unhappy pet owner then tosses the voracious eaters into local canals where they breed and make their way into larger waterways.

Allan reminded me, "Don't forget walking catfish, oscars, tegu lizards, cobras, Gambian giant rats, Nile monitors, and Siberian hybrid boars are all invading Florida."

It wasn't surprising that the cobra made it to the list. Brave thrill seekers can easily purchase venomous snakes on a variety of web sites. Venomous snakes are not cheap. A king cobra or black mamba costs a hefty $18,500.00. The deadly Gaboon viper goes for about $4,000.00. If one is low on funds, a variety of rattlesnakes can be purchased for under $500.00. Jumbo non-venomous varieties such as pythons and anacondas are sold under $200.00 on some sites. Most states have strict licensing laws governing exotic pets especially poisonous ones. But some states such as South Carolina do not.

It is easy to imagine how much care and work might be involved in owning a poisonous snake. Owners grow tired of responsibility or the novelty wears off and it's another snake set free into the swamps.

Besides the obvious threat to the eco-system, some animals pose other dangers…disease. Gambian giant rats and Siberian wild boar carry diseases that can spread into domestic animals, even humans. Wild pigs carry forty-five different bacterial, viral, and parasitic diseases. The giant rats carry the monkey pox virus, similar to small pox. The virus is usually contained to animals, mostly rodents and primates, but has managed to make its way into humans. In 2003, several states reported outbreaks from human contact with pet prairie dogs who acquired the disease from giant rats. It is not too far from the realm of reason to fear that the next great pandemic could arise from exotic foreign animals invading our forests and wetlands.

Numerous sites on the internet have blogs of complaining citizens who are outraged by the invasion of these monsters. How dare they invade our swamp! They do not belong here. The government must do something to stop them. And they are.

Miami-Dade now has a "python patrol" made up of local police, firemen, and utility workers to help round up the animals. The Florida Fish and Wildlife Conservation Commission began a special hunting season for snakes in South Florida. The hunters must be licensed and must not remove the animal from the area alive. Although some of the snakes will be captured and sent to zoos, the vast majority are killed.

There are monsters in the Everglades. They are not strange mutations or unidentified animals. Nor are they the displaced animals forced to adapt to a new environment. We capture wild animals, take them from their native environment, and force them to live in captivity. We feed them. We treat them as pets. They entertain us. When we grow tired of them, or they become too big to suit our needs, we discard them back into the wild. We decide for them their fate. Then we scream in fear when we encounter them in places they shouldn't be. We blame them for our irresponsibility. Then we hunt them, and kill them. There are indeed monsters in the Everglades.

Visitors from Afar

"I don't mind UFO's and ghost stories, it's just that I tend to give value to the storyteller rather than to the story itself." ~ Robert Stack

No mysterious city would be complete without a wide array of UFO stories. Miami seems to have its share. In April 2000, several sightings of unidentified spacecraft were reported in Miami and the nearby Everglades. One witness reported seeing a green ball of fire over the Everglades. Another witness claimed to see an aircraft covered in lights over downtown Miami that same month. One woman heard noises on her porch late one evening and claims to have seen a strange creature outside of her window. In November that same year, a man saw a flying object that resembled an upside down plate with a cup on top covered in blinking lights. Bright, shiny objects surrounded it. Miami has so many reports of UFOs and alien abductions that it has several organizations dedicated to recording such events.

One individual gave a vivid account of seeing alien visitors during a family trip to Miami. He described driving on a lonely highway in Miami with his family asleep in the car. Suddenly he witnessed what appeared to be four alien beings crossing the highway. He described the beings as wearing tight suits that covered their somewhat large, oval heads. The beings vanished into the darkness before he could gather his senses.

Countless stories of alien abduction have been recorded all around South Florida. The stories are usually very similar. Victims often report seeing a bright light or strange object outside of their home. Some have reported feeling a sensation of suffocating, and vision becoming fogged then waking in a white room. Most describe seeing gray creatures with large heads and strange eyes. Others describe the beings as somewhat reptilian.

There is usually some sort of medical examination involved. Some people have reported being cut on the hand or arm, others in the abdomen. Strange instruments are used to probe and take samples. One individual awoke in a white room accompanied by cages of animals that were also abducted and being tested. Then the abductee is returned to their bed or back yard, unharmed, but with vague memories of the abduction.

These accounts are nothing new. People from all over the world claim to have witnessed UFOs, and even encounters with extraterrestrial beings, and alien abductions. A recent poll taken by Newsweek reported that 48% of Americans believe that extraterrestrial visitors are real and that the government covers it up. But no one has had a more vivid experience with visitors from outer space than the late, great Jackie Gleason.

Jackie Gleason was born on February 26, 1916, in New York City to Irish Catholic immigrants. His father, John Herbert, was an insurance clerk who left the family when Jackie was eight-years-old. His mother died just eight years later. His only sibling, a brother, had died of tuberculosis when Jackie was three. He endured a very lonely, sad childhood.

A born entertainer, Jackie appeared in plays at church and school throughout his childhood. His first real gig was as an MC for a vaudeville club. He traveled through the Northeast performing at clubs during his early adult years and met and married a dancer, Genevieve Halford in 1936. The couple had two daughters. They separated in 1954, but Jackie, a devout Catholic, took almost twenty years to finalize the divorce.

In 1941, at the age of twenty-five, he ventured to Hollywood under a contract with Jack Warner. His early movies were less than successful so he began a television career by joining "Cavalcade of Stars" as a summer host. The show immediately signed him up on a permanent basis. It was here where he created his most memorable characters including *Ralph Kramden*.

After guest hosting a variety of shows on various networks, CBS signed Gleason up to host his own show. In the 1955-1956 season, he took the Kramden's Honeymooners and turned it into its own show. He continued to appear in movies including "The Hustler" where he performed all of the pool shots himself. The movie earned him an Oscar nomination.

In 1962, Gleason returned to television with his new "Jackie Gleason Show," filmed in Miami. Gleason originally moved to Miami because he loved to play golf and the weather allowed him to play year round.

In addition to being a great entertainer, Jackie Gleason also had an intense interest in spiritualism and the occult. William A. Henry III outlined in his book, *The Life and Legend of Jackie Gleason*, Gleason's interest in the unknown. He wrote, "Jackie Gleason had a lifelong fascination with the supernatural. He would spend small fortunes on everything from financing psychic research to buying a sealed box said to contain actual ectoplasm, the spirit of life itself. He would contact everyone from back-alley charlatans to serious researchers like J.B. Rhine of Duke University and, disdaining the elitism of the scholarly apparatus, would treat them all much the same way."

He had a fascination for UFOs and financed psychic research. His library contained over 1700 books on paranormal, occult, UFO's, and parapsychology. An insomniac, he spent many a sleepless night in his library reading books, magazine articles, and journals on the subjects. His collection included numerous books on psychics and mediums from the 1800s, Fate Magazines from the 1950s, and The Encyclopedia of Death. One periodical was The Occult Digest dating back to the early 1900s. The Jackie Gleason Collection is now owned by the University of Miami Library. Gleason's widow donated the collection after his death.

One of Gleason's close friends who shared his interest in UFOs was President Richard Nixon. Gleason, a strong supporter of the Republican Party, became friends with the president through their mutual golf interests. Nixon had a home in Biscayne Bay a short distance from Miami.

In an interview with Larry Warren, a retired U. S. Air Force Security Police Officer at RAF Bentwater in England, Gleason described a very strange encounter with President Nixon. Warren witnessed a bizarre incident in 1980 that became known as the Rendlesham Forest Incident. Numerous UFO sightings had been recorded by airmen at the base. In December, 1980, Warren had been called to investigate strange lights in the forest just outside of the base. There he and several others witnessed a grounded spacecraft of some sort. It was surrounded by a mist and brightly colored lights. Warren claimed to have witnessed some sort of meeting between the airbase commander and three beings from the ship. The incident is often referred to as the British Roswell. Warren met with Gleason in 1987 shortly before Gleason's death.

On February 19, 1973, the two had spent the day

golfing together. Many hours later, around midnight, the president showed up at Gleason's residence in a private car with no security. Nixon told Gleason that he wanted to show him something. He escorted Gleason to the car then drove him to nearby Homestead Air Force Base. Gleason described going past a number of labs, then being shown wreckage of a UFO. He was then taken to a room where he saw several large containers with glass tops. Inside were the mangled bodies of what at first appeared to be children.

"Then upon closer examination, I saw that some the other figures looked quite old. Most of them were terribly mangled as if they had been in an accident," Gleason stated.

Gleason went on to tell Warren that he was so traumatized by the experience that he didn't sleep for three weeks following the incident. For many years following the visit to Homestead Air Force Base, Gleason is said to have had numerous UFO sightings. He became convinced that there might be an underwater base of some type in the Bermuda Triangle.

No one but those present that night at the base know for certain what Jackie Gleason witnessed. Was it some prank that the president played on him knowing his belief in the supernatural and space aliens? Was the conversation he later had with Warren based on fact? Warren was convinced that Gleason was sincere. Jackie Gleason died on June

27, 1987 of heart failure. He is buried in Our Lady of Mercy Cemetery in Miami. His tombstone reads, "And away we go."

Today, the theater that bears his name, The Jackie Gleason Theater of Performing Arts, is said to be haunted by none other than Gleason himself. Many an actor has felt cold spots while performing on stage. Others have felt as if someone is watching them from behind stage. His love of Miami and performing keep him in the theater night after night. Given his strong interest in the afterlife, if anyone can walk between the world of the living and the dead, it's Jackie Gleason.

Close Encounters

"Babies have big heads and big eyes, and tiny little bodies with tiny little arms and legs. So did the aliens at Roswell! I rest my case."~William Shatner

Miami is home to an entire sub-culture of individuals who believe that extraterrestrials have communicated with them, abducted them, or are planning to rescue them from this life. Some of these believers have intertwined their belief in alien life forms with their religious beliefs.

Not all are afraid of the visitors. Various groups of believers have emerged recently in the Miami area who not only welcome the idea of extraterrestrials but some claim to be aliens themselves. The U.S. Raelian Movement is a religious order following the teachings of a former French race car magazine editor, Claude Vorhilhon. This modern day messiah, who changed his name to Rael, claims he is the messenger for beings he calls the Elohim. Rael believes he was abducted by these beings in 1973 and taken aboard their spaceship. There he learned that humans were created in a laboratory by the Elohimand placed on planet earth. The lab was destroyed many years ago but was allegedly located in Israel.

Interestingly, the word Elohim in Hebrew means "God." There have been many speculations and wide-spread attention in the 1970s and 1980s about ancient astronauts and their link to biblical references. Prehistoric carvings in stones depict astronaut looking beings indicating that early aliens landed on earth many years ago. Many ancient structures lend themselves to the possibility of a higher technology than what was available being responsible for their existence. Ancient Mayan texts describe wise beings that descended from the sky who were technically advanced.

The Old Testament is believed by some to describe visitors from outer space. Many believe that the God and Angels described in the Bible are actually extraterrestrial beings.

And it came to pass on the third day in the morning, that there were thunders and lightnings, and a thick cloud upon the mount, and the voice of the trumpet exceeding loud; so that all the people that was in the camp trembled.

And Moses brought forth the people out of the camp to meet with God; and they stood at the nether part of the mount.

And Mount Sinai was altogether on a smoke, because the LORD descended upon it in fire: and the smoke thereof ascended as the smoke of a furnace, and the whole mount quaked greatly. Exodus 19:16-18

Ancient Astronaut theorists contend that alien beings came to earth millions of years ago. The beings' DNA was similar to humans. These beings bred with humans creating hybrid humans. These hybrids in turn worshipped the beings as God and Angels.

There were giants in the earth in those days; and also after that, when the sons of God came in unto the daughters of men, and they bare children to them, the same became mighty men which were of old, men of renown. Genesis 6:4

There are numerous references in the bible to "chariots of fire" that many theorists claim are descriptions of space ships.

"...there appeared a chariot of fire, and horses of fire, and parted them both asunder; and Elijah went up by a whirlwind into heaven." 2 Kings 2:11

The Bible is not the only sacred text where these references are found. Other religions record similar events using the same descriptions. In Erich von Daniken's bestseller, <u>Chariots of the Gods</u>, the author wrote, "the 'fiery heavenly chariots', described by

Enoch and Elijah are also found in Buddhist (Padmasambhava) and Hindu (Ardjuna) mythology. Apparently every child in India is well aware of ancient flying gods and their aircraft, which they called Vimanas."

Wernher Von Braun, a German rocket scientist who eventually worked with NASA, once said, "Our sun is one of a 100 billion stars in our galaxy. Our galaxy is one of billions of galaxies populating the universe. It would be the height of presumption to think that we are the only living thing in that enormous immensity."

Some believers have a different take; they believe that alien beings inhabit their bodies. They believe that they were born as humans but during abduction the aliens replaced the human soul or share the body with the original soul. One man who called himself *Aldin* said that he and his partner just woke up one day and everything looked different. The two believe that they've experienced some sort of rebirth.

One Miami man, Tony Diaz, told a reporter, "I'm not from this earth."

Diaz told the reporter that he shares his body with an alien "walk in." He has hundreds of followers in the Miami area. He described his initial encounter with the aliens. Extraterrestrial visits began during his childhood in Cuba. He described ghost-like beings with large heads and almond shaped eyes. His parents thought he had mental problems and brought Tony to a psychiatrist when he was seven-years-old.

Despite his Parents' efforts, Tony had visitations from what he calls "grays" his entire life. He recalled one such visit where he was taken onto an aircraft and probed with needles. He believes that some sort of communication device was implanted in him.

Tony Diaz believes that his mission on earth is to heal. He claims to have healed people of various ailments. To his followers, he is sent from God.

The most publicized Miami abduction case was in January 1979. Filiberto Cardenas was travelling with his friend, his friend's wife, and their young daughter. They were driving through Hialeah when the car engine quit abruptly. When the men got out to inspect the engine they saw bright lights upon them. Cardenas suddenly felt paralyzed and began to levitate towards the lights. His friend watched in horror as Cardenas lifted out of sight. Cardenas was missing for over two hours. Police found him ten miles away on the Tamiami Trail. The police report cited the incident as a "close encounter of a third kind." Later under hypnosis, Cardenas gave vivid recollection of being taken to an underwater facility by aliens. Regardless of what others may think of them, these people truly believe that their experiences with aliens are real. Many of them have sought professional help and recount details of their encounters under hypnosis. For many of them, the only proof they own is drawings of spaceships and little gray men. For some of us, they are just stories, for others it is reality. No one can prove nor disprove it. All that is known is that there are many of them claiming to have these experiences. And a large number of them are living in Miami.

The Mystery of Coral Castle

"'Mad' is a term we use to describe a man who is obsessed with one Idea and nothing else." ~ Ugo Betti

One of Miami's weirdest mysteries is Coral Castle located in Homestead, 26 miles south of the city. The strange structure was built in 1923 by Edward Leedskalnin, an immigrant from Latvia. The castle was built as a tribute to a young woman he had hoped to marry, sixteen-year-old Agnes Scuffs. Agnes felt he was too old and too poor for her and broke off the engagement just days before the wedding leaving Leedskalnin heartbroken. Not too long afterwards, the jilted Leedskalnin left his native country and made his home in South Florida. He never married nor did he ever recover from the rejection. He spent the remainder of his days building his Coral Castle.

Although no one really knows for sure what prompted Ed Leedskalnin to build the castle. He was a small man, only five feet tall and weighed about one hundred pounds. He had only a fourth grade education. Somehow he managed to single-handedly build it with only hand-made tools. By all modern standards, the task is physically impossible.

He worked only at night allowing no one to see how he shaped or moved the gigantic coral slabs, each weighing approximately 15 to 30 tons. He hand carved the coral into geometric shapes, shapes of planets, moon phases, and occult symbols. In twenty five years, he alone quarried and carved 1100 tons of coral rock.

His carvings include a 22-ton moon symbol, a 22-ton obelisk, a 23-ton Jupiter block, a 9-ton gate and a 3-ton rocking chair. Both the gate and chair move with the pressure of a finger. His lens-less telescope is 25 feet high. His pool was circular to symbolize the moon. A fully operating sundial calibrated to the winter and summer solstices told accurate time.

Only once did he ask for help. In 1936, he moved the structure ten miles. He hired a tractor to assist but would not allow the driver to see how he moved the coral. The driver arrived in the mornings after the heavy coral was situated on the flatbed trailers.

Leedskalnin claimed to move the coral with the use of magnets. Researchers found several energy vortices within the vicinity of the castle. He wrote numerous pamphlets on his use of energy, magnets, and electricity. In his pamphlets on magnets, *Magnetic Current*, he wrote, "First I will describe what a magnet is. You have seen straight bar magnets, U shape magnets, sphere or ball magnets and Alnico magnets in many shapes, and usually a hole in the middle. In all magnets one end of the metal is North Pole and the other South Pole, and those which have no end one side is North Pole and the other South Pole."

Leedskalnin went to talk of the earth as a giant magnet. He noted, "The earth itself is a great big magnet. In general these North and South Pole individual magnets are circulating in the same way as in the permanent magnet metal."

In his pamphlets he goes into intricate detail on how to conduct specific experiments with not only magnets but electricity. He claimed to know little about electricity until he began his experiments. Ed Leedskalnin wrote these pamphlets not for the average reader, but as instructional manuals to those who wanted to conduct the experiments. He never revealed how he moved or shaped the coral rock that he used to build the castle. He died of cancer in December 1951 taking his secrets with him.

Many theories have arisen through the years attempting to explain how he did it. One such theory claims neighbors witnessed him moving the stones. They described him placing his hands on the stones, singing some sort of chant, then levitating them. In one article in *Fate Magazine*, witnesses are cited as having seen him "float" the coral rocks in the air.

In the article, "Coral Castle," writer Frank Josep wrote, "Alternative science investigators suggest that Leedskalnin somehow learned the secret of the 'world grid,' an invisible pattern of energy lines surrounding the Earth which concentrates points of telluric power where they intersect. It was here, at one of these intersections of Earth energy, that he was supposedly able to move his prodigious stone blocks using the unseen power of our planet. In fact, in *The Enigma of Coral Castle*, Ray Stoner suggests that Leedskalnin moved the Castle not because it was threatened by an encroaching subdivision, but because a surveying error misplaced the site ten miles from an Earth energy vortex or focal point. In order for the structures to maximize this energy, the entire complex needed to be relocated in Homestead, where the telluric forces were focused."

Bruce Cathe, author of *The Energy Grid*, stated that he believed not only the grid was responsible for Ed's ability to create the castle but also responsible for alleged UFO sightings in the area. Ed believed he discovered the secrets of ancient pyramids. Ed also claimed to see beads of light that he believed represented pure energy.

In a Miami Herald article from Halloween 2001, Phoebe Flowers suggested that the castle was haunted. One of the castle's employees stated in an interview that there was one area of the building that he perceived as negative energy. He directed the journalist to a small room downstairs in the castle tower. On the door reads a sign, "Some of Ed's Heavy Tools."He pointed to a corner in the room and said, "There is evil in this corner."

He asked Flowers to stand in the corner with her eyes closed and facing the wall where Ed's tool hung. She described the experience as "a little too much like Blair Witch for comfort."

Ray told her to let the energy in the corner move her where it wants. She began to feel something pulling her and she swayed back and forth. It's hard to say if the energy felt there is caused from the magnetic energy present or the ghost of Ed, perhaps both. There is some speculation that the electromagnetic currents that he used may have caused Ed's cancer.

During my visit to the castle I did feel a strange current of energy within. Apparently Ed enjoyed the outdoors because just about everything there including the bed and bathtub are outside. The only indoor areas are Ed's work shed and a small upstairs room used for storage. The room contained strange hanging devices that he had used to assist in moving the coral. Some believe that he also slept in that room on occasion. Also in the room is an eerie life-sized photograph of Ed. Most of the "pulling" energy seems to gravitate around that photograph.

I couldn't help but notice that no matter where I stood in that room, Ed's eyes seemed to follow me. At one point, I yelled to him across the room, "Ed, you are really creepy aren't you?"

It was at that point that the battery door on my camera opened itself and my batteries fell out and rolled down the stairs. After recovering the batteries, I went back up and apologized to Ed. Although I felt nothing malevolent in the castle, it does have an interestingly different vibration from others places I have investigated. Maybe it's just the residual energy from Ed's unrequited love for Agnes and the feelings of rejection from which he never recovered.

The Lady in Blue

"The place is very well and quiet and the children only scream in a low voice." ~ Lord Byron

No doubt one of the most popular urban legends is Bloody Mary. The story has many variations but the end result is always the same. I remember as a kid standing alone in front of the bathroom mirror with a flashlight and staring into my own eyes, repeating her name three times. Then of course tossing the light and running screaming out of the darkened room.

The original Bloody Mary is a folktale from England. Some believe she is the ghost of a girl named Mary Worth. Some versions of the story claim that she was in a terrible accident leaving her face disfigured. She spent a very long time, and some references say years, others months, refusing to look at her reflection in the mirror. Then finally, late one evening, she brought a candle into the bathroom and finally saw her face. She became so hysterical, she committed suicide. Other versions claim Mary Worth was a child killer and went mad after she killed her own children. Another source cited that she was only accused of killing her children which caused her to commit suicide.

In Long Island, New York, another Mary tale emerged leading curiosity seekers to her grave to summon her. Again, there are many variations of the story but it's a more modern version of the classic Mary legend. One version of the Long Island Mary story tells of a young girl raped by her abusive father. Young Mary became pregnant and her father forced her to have the child. The beatings and rape continued to the point of driving the poor girl mad. She is said to have killed herself and her baby in the barn of her father's home. The ghost part of the legend states that the apparition of Mary carrying her baby is seen along the highways late at night.

Some versions of the Long Island Mary say that she was hanged by locals for witchcraft and she cursed the town before her death. A popular version of the legend tells of a teenage Mary who is killed by her jealous boyfriend who pushed her from a moving car. After the fall, Mary pulls herself up and runs into the street and is hit by another car. Mary's grave site is said to be in the Sweet Hollow Road Cemetery in Long Island. I visited the area a few years ago but no one could tell me exactly where the grave was located.

The Mary legend is paralleled in some ways to a Latin legend, La Llorana, "the Weeping Woman." The origins of this legend, like the Mary legend, are unknown but the story has spun around Mexico, Central America, and the Southwest U.S. for generations. A popular account tells of a beautiful young woman named Maria. She married a very wealthy man and had two sons. In time, her husband became abusive and eventually left Maria for a woman of higher social standing. Her former husband visited the children but shunned Maria. She became jealous not only of his new bride but his attention for the boys.

One evening as Maria walked with her boys near the river, a carriage came upon them. It was the boys' father and his new wife. He spoke to his children ignoring Maria then drove away. Maria is said to have gone into a blind rage and killed her children by drowning them in the river. When she realized what she had done, she ran through the town crying and wailing. She spent the remainder of life mourning the loss of her children. She was still a young woman when her frail body was found dead at the river's edge. Soon thereafter stories of her ghost wandering the riverfront began to emerge. She became known as La Llorana. The legends say that she continues to wander the dark nights in search of more children to murder.

In Miami, the homeless children seem to have combined both the original Bloody Mary legend with La Llorana. They often interchange the names, but they've added a new twist on the old legends. The children believe that there is a spiritual warfare going on in Miami. Angels of God fight Satan who has teamed up with Bloody Mary to consume the souls of the children. Often the homeless are left to sleep in the streets and the neon of South Beach is comforting to the children. They believe that angels eat light in order to fly. Satan and his demons enter Miami through doors from hell and wage war on mankind. For generations, a popular local legend tells of the entrance to hell. The evil gateway is supposedly somewhere Interstate Highway 75 and Highway 826. In a tunnel, it is said that teenagers have ventured in, never to return. Strange writings on the wall warn not proceed. The passage gets darker and narrower as it winds further down. The children believe that Satan and his demons disappear into this dark passage and travel beneath the ground. The demons feed on negative emotions, such as fear and hate. The fiercest demon is Bloody Mary. The children say she cries blood from her empty eye sockets and feeds on children. The children believe that if you awaken in the night and see her ghoulish apparition that soon you will die. Stories of her circulate through the streets and homeless shelters. As with the original Bloody Mary legends, she appears in a mirror and breaks through the glass. Even the toughest of them believe it is true. One child told a reporter, "But even gangs think Bloody Mary is real." One young boy described "Bloody Mary made a pact with Satan: She had killed her own child and had made a secret vow to kill all human children."

Another boy in Little Haiti reported, "I know a boy who learned to sleep with his eyes open, but she burned through a shelter wall to get him! When the people found him, he was all red with blood."

He warned, "You got to be careful! If she sees you, she can hunt you forever. She's in Miami! And she knows our face."

Homeless children are often moved from one place to another with little time to settle anywhere. Nothing is ever permanent for them. They meet other children suffering their same plight unable to form lasting bonds with them. These are the secret stories they tell each other through the dark, scary nights. These children spend their lives merely trying to survive. Violence and death are all around them especially at night. To many of them, it seems God has abandoned them. Angels hide deep in the Everglades appearing only to defend the truly good. One angel who is the greatest protector of children is called the Blue Lady. She has dark hair, tan skin, and blue eyes. She appears to her believers and guides them away from evil. The children say that she lives in the ocean and her name is secret. She appears to and protects those who call her name. She gives them hope.

It's highly likely that the protective Blue Lady is derived from the Santeria Orisha, Yemaya. In all Afro-Caribbean traditions, she lives in the ocean and is the protector of children. The great mother is loving, compassionate, and protects her children from the demons. She is dressed in blue and white and often appears shrouded in bright light. She, along with an army of angels and the spirits of dead relatives, are who the children pray to for protection. They believe that once a spirit sees your face, they can always find you.

According to the children, the deceased appear as they were in life, surrounded by colored light. They, as well as the Blue Lady, bring messages to console and protect them. Despite the horrors that surround them on a daily basis, many of the children strive to be good, believing it strengthens these spirits who protect them. These kids also have their own version of heaven. It's a beautiful jungle guarded by large crocodiles who only allow the children in. In order to enter, the child must drop a fresh palm leaf on the grave of a loved one.

The odd thing is that usually urban legends are passed down word of mouth through families and communities. These children travel from place to place. The fact that they all have the same version of the story is eerie. What makes it unusual is that for the homeless children, these stories come to them from the mouths of spirits. This is what baffles folklorists. These homeless children speak from actual experience in witnessing spiritual visitations. One boy said that his cousin's spirit appeared to him, warning, "Stay strong and smart so's you count on yourself, no one else. Never stop watching. Bloody Mary is coming with Satan. And she's seen your face."

A seven-year-old girl described her experience with the Blue Lady, "She's a magic lady, nice and pretty and smart! She lives in the ocean and comes just to kids."

The spirit appeared to the girl after she was brutally beaten by her drunk father. The father had eaten the last of their food and the girl's mother got angry. The child had tried to break up a fight between her parents in an abandoned building. She was hit in the forehead. She said, "I tried to sleep so my head and stomach would stop hurting, but they kept hurting."

During the night, a window shattered and there appeared a woman dressed in blue, with white, pink, and gold flowers draped over her arms. She described the encounter, "My head was hurting, but she touched it and her hand was cool like ice. She said she's my friend always."

The President of the International Society for Contemporary Legend Research, Bill Ellis stated in an article, "Myths Over Miami," Miami New Times, 1997, "Whenever you ask children where they first heard one of their myths, you get answers that are impossible clues: 'A friend's friend read it in a paper; a third cousin told me.' When a child says he got the story from the spirit world, as homeless children do, you've hit the ultimate non sequitur."

Taking into consideration the spiritual activity in Miami, not just the spirits of the dead, but spirits of the deities of the ancient traditions practiced here, there exists spirits who protect these children. Someone has to.

Haunted Highway

"That fateful stretch of road has since been dubbed the Highway of Death."--John Whitehead

Some of my favorite haunted stories come from Key West. Key West is one hundred fifty four miles from Miami. The drive from Miami to Key West is a monotonous one traveling over one hundred miles of tiny islands and bridges. Ghostly images and zombie-like specters haunt this lonely highway retelling the tales of tragedies that took their lives.

In 1912 Henry Flagler had succeeded in building his railroad that reached all the way to Key West. He believed it profitable allowing better access to the Caribbean. The venture had taken seven years and 5,000 men to complete. Flagler died a year after its completion.

On September 1, 1935, Labor Day, storm warnings spread across South Florida and the Keys. Residents began attempts to protect properties by boarding up windows and securing boats. They prepared for the loss of electricity and stockpiled food and drinking water. By mid-afternoon that day an evacuation of the islands were ordered. When local authorities contacted those on the mainland they received no reply. Lines of communication were already hindered by the rapidly approaching storm. Finally emergency messages made it through and a train was sent from Miami to assist in the evacuation. But the train was late leaving the city. It was 9:00 PM when the train finally reached the middle keys. Hundreds of people boarded in an effort to escape. It was four hours later when the train finally made its way into Islamorada. By now the storm had already hit land. Those who didn't make it to the train attempted to gain safety by tying themselves to palm trees. As the massive storm struck land, ten passenger cars were thrown about and the train tracks ripped from their foundations.

On Tuesday morning, many smaller islands had completely disappeared. Those who were tied in trees were tossed around like ragdolls, their bodies now twisted around the trees. Many corpses were tossed into nearby swamps. Others had washed out to sea. Hundreds lost their lives in the storm and over four hundred bodies were never found. The railroad was never rebuilt.

In Greg Jenkins book, *Florida's Ghostly Legends and Haunted Folklore: South and Central Florida, Volume 1*, a local fisherman recounted a story from his boyhood in 1943. He and another boy were shrimping off the side of the road beneath a bridge when they noticed a storm was coming upon them. Lightning began to flash and they saw a wall of rain in a distance. The boys decided to gather their belongings and head for safety. Before they could get their shoes on and pull in their nets, large drops of rain began to fall which rapidly turned into heavy rain. As the boys climbed up onto the bank they grabbed a piece of old metal track. Suddenly a bolt of lightning struck so close that the boys felt their hair stand on ends. They ducked back down fearing being struck. As they huddled down under the bridge they heard a strange sound, a train whistle. The boy peeked up over the bridge and pulled back under the pillions quickly. He stared at his friend blankly then told him what he had seen: a train was heading straight towards them! The old railroad tracks were rocking and the train sounded louder and louder. The two then realized that there were no train tracks ahead; the train would crash. They huddled closer together as the sound of the train roared above them. The boys covered their faces and prepared for the great crash. Then the sound of the train faded away and the whistle quieted. They looked ahead and saw only the rain and some lightning in the distance. There was no train, there never had been; only the ghostly impression of the phantom train that still runs through Islamorada.

    The ghost train is not the only reminder of the hurricane of 1935. Many have reported seeing a phantom car driving down the road late at night. One woman in the 1980s was walking her dog one early morning. She saw an old car that she described as black and at least fifty-years-old with dim headlights. She heard the putter of an old engine. Her dog barked and whimpered as the antiquated vehicle drove past them. She saw the silhouette of a driver inside. As the car travelled over the bridge it faded into the fog, its rear tail lights disappearing. At first she thought that maybe the car had stopped. She watched expecting to see the driver appear. But the car was gone.

Herds of shadowy figures are seen wandering aimless from the marshes and estuaries on stormy nights. Shortly before Hurricane Andrew made landfall in 1992, hundreds of zombie-like figures were seen staggering northbound along Highway 1. Their shadowy hunched-over silhouettes emerged from the marshes; fading in and out as they relived their attempts to evacuate from the islands. These restless spirits serve as a reminder of the devastation brought about by the Hurricane of 1935.

Island of Bones

"The ocean moans over dead men's bones."--
Thomas Bailey Aldrich

Key West is an amazing place. Upon first entering the island, it looks like any other seaside resort town; hotels, beautiful homes, and historic landmarks. Suddenly one finds himself in Old Town and it's like stepping back in time on some lost Caribbean island. Cypress wood cottages adorned with tin roofs line its narrow streets. Ferrell chickens and roosters run wild, left over from the days when cockfighting was legal. Like a Caribbean Island, the pace is slow and laid back. Like Texas, "it's a whole other country." And it was at one time.

On April 23, 1982 the U.S. Border Patrol set up a barricade on Highway 1 forcing residents of the Keys to prove their citizenship before entering the mainland. This outraged the residents as well as the mayor of Key West. The mayor and other islanders attempted to file an injunction to stop the blockade but their efforts were to no avail. So Key West did the next best thing; it seceded from the Union.

At noon the following day, Key West and the rest of the Florida Keys seceded from the Union and announced that the country called Conch Republic was independent from the United States. They waged war on Naval personnel by throwing stale

Cuban bread at them. After one minute of rebelling, the Conch Republic surrendered to the Naval Station in Key West. The republic then demanded one billion dollars in relief to rebuild their country. Today, residents are considered duel citizens of the United States and the Conch Republic.

But this island paradise has another side to it. Behind the myriad restaurants, hotels, music venues, and T-shirt shops of Key West lies a dark and ghastly past. This quaint island paradise has a death-laden history leaving behind some of the most intriguing haunted tales. Early Native American tribes originally inhabited the island but were killed by warring tribes. The dead were left scattered all over the beach. When the Spanish arrived in the 16th they found the island covered in human bones giving way to the name, Cayo Hueso, meaning "Bone Key."

The Key West cemetery is located in the middle of the island. Like the New Orleans' Cities of The Dead, the Key West cemetery is above-ground. Unlike New Orleans, the tomb style was not adapted due to soft ground and rising coffins. The ground in Key West is very hard making it impossible to bury beneath the ground.

The first cemetery was on the beach at the Southernmost Point. A hurricane in 1847 disinterred most of the bodies. The disturbed corpses were flung all over the tiny island, some hanging in trees. Some bodies were never identified. This forced the islanders to move the burial ground to the harder ground in the island's center. The local joke is that the cemetery is "dead center."

The twenty acre cemetery was built in 1847 and has tombs for about 60,000 internments; 100,000 are buried there, some with no headstones. Some tombs are in extremely poor condition. Some of the older concrete slabs are rising out of the ground. Some tombs have tilted headstones, others are cracked open completely and overgrown with weeds.

One of the oldest tombs in the cemetery belongs to a husband and wife who died on the same day, a murder/suicide. A large monument honoring those who died on the USS Maine sits nearby. The USS Maine blew up in Havana Harbor on February 15, 1989. Two hundred sixty Americans were killed. Only about two dozen are actually buried in the tomb.

The Otto Family plot is not only the final resting place for the family but the family pets as well. Three Yorkshire Terriers and a tamed pet deer, Elfina, share the plot with their loving owners. Minnie Otto's epitaph reads "Her life was a beautiful morning."

Several tombs have humorous epitaphs inscribed. Edwina Lariz's tomb reads, "Devoted Fan of Singer Julio Inglesias." Gloria M. Russell final message states, "I'm Just Resting My Eyes." But the best one is the tomb of B.P. (Pearl) Roberts, the village hypochondriac. It reads, "I Told You I Was Sick."

Passersby claim to see apparitions wandering about in the cemetery late at night. Voices are heard within its walls. Perhaps it's the dismal cries of the forgotten ones buried within. A mysterious Bahamian woman often appears yelling at visitors if they lean on a tomb or happen to walk on a gravesite. She watches to make sure those who visit are being respectful to those buried there.

A few blocks past the cemetery is the oldest Catholic church in Florida, Mary Immaculate Star of The Sea, which dates back to 1852. In 1992 a nun built the grotto to Our Lady of Lourdes in memory of the 800 people who died in the Atlantic-Gulf Hurricane of 1919.

Our Lady of Lourdes refers to the apparition of Mary who appeared in 1858 to a young girl named Bernadette in a cave Lourdes, France. Sister Mary Louis Gabriel built the grotto to protect the island from ever suffering a direct hit from a hurricane. Thus far, the grotto has done its job.

The Key West lighthouse has its own ghost story. In 1832 when caretaker Michael Mabrity died from yellow fever, his wife, Barbara Mabrity, took over his role. She was one of two female lighthouse caretakers in the area. In nearby Sand Key, Rebecca Flaherty had taken over that lighthouse when her husband passed away. She lived on the property with her five children. Both women could see the lights from the other's tower.

By noon on a warm October day, 1846, Barbara had completed her daily chores on the tower. Each day required her to turn down wicks on the oil lamps, and clean them thoroughly. She emptied the whale oil out of each draining it into a clean container. She cleaned and polished each of the fifteen lamps carefully refilling the oil. The previous evening's insects attracted into the tower needed to be swept out. She diligently repeated the morning ritual each day. On that day however, something was different. It was unseasonably warm with no breeze present.

Barbara had lived in the Keys long enough to familiarize herself with weather patterns. She knew on that morning, this was merely the calm before the storm. She remained unconcerned despite the dark horizon looming over the gulf. She had survived three hurricanes with no major damage to the tower so she went about her business as usual.

By morning on October 10, 1846, raging winds and torrential rain pounded the island. Barbara, her six children, and residents of the island sought shelter in the lighthouse tower. On Sand Key, Rebecca Flaherty and her children did the same.

The angry storm pummeled the Keys. Sand Key along with the lighthouse and the Flaherty family disappeared from the map. Key West was devastated. The lighthouse tower and the caretaker's cottage were obliterated. The residents seeking shelter there along with all of the Mabrity children were killed. Miraculously, Barbara survived.

The grief stricken widow having nothing left opted to continue doing all that she knew, take care of the lighthouse. She remained its caretaker until 1864. She was fired at eighty-two-years-old for making negative comments about the Union. She died three years later.

The ghost of Barbara Mabrity is heard walking up and down the steps of tower early in the morning. She continues her daily rituals of cleaning and caring for the lighthouse that sits on the property today. On stormy nights, the screams and cries of lost souls echo through the howling wind.

Spirits of Key West

"Our dead are never dead to us, until we have forgotten them." ~ George Eliot

With so much death in such a small area, it's no surprise that so many homes and businesses in Key West have colorful characters haunting about. One of the more tragic ones is the son of William Curry, Florida's first millionaire. He built a beautiful mansion on Duval Street as a wedding gift for his son Robert. Robert had been sickly all of his life with asthma and other random illnesses. His father wanted to provide for him in any way he could; given his ill health.

Robert didn't have the business mind of his father. Between failing health and on and off bouts of depression, he found himself constantly in dire-straights financially. Unable to cope with his misfortunes, Robert ultimately committed suicide by hanging himself in the upstairs bathroom in 1917.

The home was sold to the Order of Elks. One evening, a custodian was in the building alone finishing up his chores. As he completed his inspection of the first floor, he heard slow, methodical footsteps going up the stairs, then a loud crash coming from the second floor. Believing someone was in the building with him, he raced upstairs calling out to whoever might be there. He turned on the lights only to find himself in the building alone. Much to his surprise a large table was completely flipped over.

The building later became an Italian restaurant. One resident of the island recalled an encounter with the ghost when he was a teenager. He and some friends were outside of the mansion when all three of them witnessed a man appearing in the third floor window. The figure leaned against the glass glaring out at them from above. The boys saw his eyes which glowed yellow then the figure vanished.

Another resident who actually lived in an apartment above the restaurant recalled problems while attempting to hang pictures on the walls. All of his pictures were hung with no problem except one of a boat. Every time he hung the picture on the wall and walked away, it would fall to the floor. After numerous attempts, the picture was finally thrown off, slamming against the floor breaking the glass.

Today the building is home to Hard Rock Café. Employees report a sense of being watched on the third floor where the administrative offices. On the second floor, where Robert hanged himself, a cold chill can often be experienced. It can only be assumed that Robert never left the house, and probably doesn't plan to anytime soon.

A few blocks down from the Hard Rock Café is Captain Tony's Saloon, Key West's first bar. It is the original location for Sloppy Joe's of Key West, a favorite hangout of Ernest Hemingway. Long before the location became a bar, it was the site of the first mortuary in Key West. The original building sat next to a large oak tree used for hangings in the early days of the island. Today, the building has expanded and was built around the hanging tree which now grows up through the center of the bar. Seventy-five people were hanged ranging from common murderers to pirates. But one executed murderer is said to still haunt the building.

The nameless ghost is said to wander the bar still wearing the blue nightgown she wore the night she was hanged. As the legend goes, the woman went mad one night and brutally murdered her husband and two children in their home as they slept. Outraged neighbors dragged her of her bed and brought her to justice at the hanging tree. But rather than snapping her neck, the rope tightened only enough to slowly strangle her. It took over an hour for her to die. It's said her face turned as blue as her gown.

When the building was expanded and the foundation replaced, sixteen skeletons were found under the original foundation and in the walls. During the original construction, a hurricane had struck pulling up many bodies from their beachside graves. Some of them were thrown into the partially constructed frame of the building. But rather than remove them, they were concreted into the structure.

The grave of the funeral director's daughter, Elvira, is still intact as part of the flooring of the bar. Beneath the hanging tree is a headstone from the grave of Reba Sawyer who died in 1950. She's not buried there however. After her death, Reba's husband discovered that she had been having an affair for over ten years. Love letters left behind in the dead woman's belongings gave away the sordid details of her rendezvous with her lover which usually included a visit to the bar. The distraught husband dumped the headstone in front of the bar one evening and yelled, "She wanted to be here so much, now she can be here for all eternity."

The bar owner decided to have the stone cemented into the floor as part of the décor.

A friendly ghost haunts the Marrero Guest Mansion. The mansion was built in 1889 by Francisco Marrero, a Cuban cigar producer. He built the home in the hopes that his love, a beautiful woman named Enriquetta, would marry him and relocate to Key West. In time, she did. The couple enjoyed a blissful life eventually having eight children.

Unbeknownst to Enriquetta, Francisco had a secret that remained in Cuba. He had a first wife that he never divorced. The matter seemed of little consequence to him during his life. Unfortunately, his life was cut short unexpectedly on a business trip to Cuba. A heartbroken Enriquetta was left to raise eight children alone and care for the house and business. She remained strong and handled things as best she could, especially for the children's sake. Then one day, the first Mrs. Marrero appeared in Key West with legal proof that both the business and the house were rightfully hers. A bitter lawsuit ensued between the two widows.

On June 16, 1891, the court made its decision. The first Mrs. Marerro, being the legal wife, was granted possession of the business and the house along with all its furnishings. Enriquetta and her children were left penniless and faced eviction from the property. Upon her eviction, Enriquetta made a promise that she would never leave the property in spirit. The first wife sold all of the property and returned to Cuba. One by one Enriquetta and her children lost their lives to tuberculosis and diphtheria. But Enriquetta's promise was never broken. It seems that she did return to the home in spirit.

Previous owners reported electrical devices turning on and off on their own. If Enriquetta doesn't like a particular guest, the chandelier in the foyer begins to swing back and forth. She's even scared a few guests away. One individual who seemed to have a nasty attitude about him experienced his key breaking off in the lock, the bathtub overflowing, and a light bulb blowing out. Other guests have smelled her lavender perfume, some even report having seen her out of the corner of their eye. Enriquetta kept her promise. To her, the house is still her home.

St. Paul's Episcopal Church sits in the middle of Old Town on Duval Street amidst music clubs, shops, and bars. The property was originally owned by the widow of John William Charles Fleming, one of the island's founding fathers. When she sold the property she insisted on one thing, that her husband's grave remain in the small cemetery located there. The church has been rebuilt four times due to natural disasters.

At one time a Baptist church sat across the alley from St. Paul's. But in 1866 a fire destroyed it completely. The minister of St. Paul's discovered his wife was having an affair with the deacon of the Baptist church. In a fit of rage, he burned the church to the ground with his wife and her Sunday school class inside. The ghosts of the children are said to be seen sometimes huddling in the garden near the cemetery. The children become upset if visitors smoke in the courtyard garden.

Another ghost on the property is that of an old Seaman that was buried in the cemetery. He's a malevolent spirit who has physically attacked visitors wandering near his gravesite. There is no documentation as to his identity. It is highly likely that this unhappy spirit is the ghost of a pirate or a sea captain captured and killed by pirates. Notorious pirate Black Caesar frequented Key West burying much of his stolen treasure there. Pirates, especially Black Caesar, customarily killed someone to be buried along with the treasure so that their ghost would guard it. An already existing cemetery makes for an excellent hiding place for buried riches… and a dead body.

Club Chameleon sits beside St. Paul's where once did the Baptist Church. The building is boarded up and covered with old building permits that are long since expired. Legend says that workmen refused to complete renovations after experiencing paranormal activity inside. Their materials and tools have remained in the building for years. Visitors claim to hear footsteps and voices coming from within. One visitor posted a photo of the club on the internet. What looks like flames are covering the exterior of the club. Today locals believe the building is cursed. Why else would a multi-million dollar property remain vacant and partially renovated a block off the main street of Old Town? For now, we are left with only speculation and stories of ghosts from a tragic fire that took the lives of so many innocents.

Memories of Papa

"Madame, all stories, if continued far enough, end in death, and he is no true-story teller who would keep that from you." ~ Ernest Hemingway

Nobel Prize winning author, Ernest Hemingway made his home in Key West. A number of establishments claim that his ghost makes his home there. Hemingway and his wife, Pauline, arrived in Key West in 1928 returning from a cruise. Casa Antigua was then the Trev-Mor Hotel, right above a Ford dealership on the first floor. The Hemingways lived in the hotel for seven weeks while waiting for a car he had ordered to drive them up North. It was in this small hotel that he wrote *A Farewell to Arms*. It was here that Ernest Hemingway fell in love with the island calling it "The St. Tropez of the poor."

Employees of Casa Antigua believe that Hemingway's ghosts stops in from time to time. No one is really sure if the resident ghost is that of Hemingway or perhaps some other spirit that merely wandered in. The locals call the ghost "The Watcher" because that's all he does. He is described as a large man standing in a doorway of what is now a gift shop. During its day as an auto shop, several men were killed when a battery exploded in the garage. The ghost could be that of the man who was killed in that accident. Regardless of who the ghost is, the one thing that is certain is that Casa Antigua is not the only location claiming to be the home of Hemingway's ghost.

One of Hemingway's favorite hangouts is the famous Sloppy Joe's Saloon. Known for his heavy drinking, the writer spent many an afternoon socializing at the bar with island locals and other writers. Hemingway's Sloppy Joe's was located at 428 Green Street, location of today's Captain Tony's Saloon. Joe Russell, a local charter fisherman and businessman, started the saloon at the end of prohibition. He and Hemingway became friends after Joe cashed a royalty check that the bank refused to honor. It was Hemingway who persuaded Russell to name the bar "Sloppy Joe's" after a Jose Garcia Rio Havana club which sold not only liquor but seafood. The ice on the seafood would melt and wet the floors of the Cuban club. A patron once told Jose that he ran a "sloppy business" thus the name Sloppy Joe. Sloppy Joe's of Key West opened in 1933, making it the oldest licensed saloon in Florida.

Ernest Hemingway was known for sticking to a strict schedule. He woke every day at dawn. His office was located in his pool house where he wrote on an old wooden desk. Every day at 3:30 PM, he would stop writing and meet his friends at Sloppy Joe's. Many of his local friends became the models of some of his most memorable characters in his stories.

Joe Russell and his saloon on Greene Street were immortalized as the fictional "Freddie" owner of Freddie's Bar and captain of the Queen Conch in

Hemingway's *To Have or Have Not*. A Cuban fisherman, Carlos Guitierrez, was the prototype for Santiago in *The Old Man and The Sea*.

It was also at Sloppy Joe's that Hemingway met a writer, Martha Gelhorn. Miss Gelhorn paid Skinner, the bartender, twenty dollars to introduce her to Hemingway. One year later, the two met again in Spain while writing about the Spanish Civil War. It was there that their relationship took root.

Many a visitor has been surprised by a man yelling to get off of his bar stool. Hemingway had a favorite bar stool and he appears at the old Sloppy Joe's and gets very upset if someone is sitting in "his" stool.

The haunted La Concha Hotel has a Hemingway Suite named in honor of the writer who often rented the corner suite on the fifth floor, room 563. He used the room for writing but more often for philandering. While still married to Pauline, he began an affair with Martha Gelhorn. He rented the suite for her to visit him in Key West.

Guests staying in the Hemingway Suite report strange happenings in the room late at night. One man kept being awakened by a VCR being thrown off of table. After the machine hit the floor for the third time, the guest lay awake all night, watching to see what was the cause. He saw the silhouette of a man hunched over in the corner, suddenly the VCR hurled to the floor once again. The man jumped up and turned on his light expecting to see an intruder only to find that he was alone. Other guests report feeling a presence; some even requesting another room because they feel they are not alone there.

The most common place to find the ghost of Ernest Hemingway is at his former home, now a museum. The Hemingway Home and Museum at 907 Whitehead Street is not only the home of the ghost of the great writer but to over forty polydactyl cats. Normal cats have eighteen toes, five on each front paw, four on each back. Polydactyl cats have as many as six or seven toes on either front or back paws. These feline mutants were favored by sailors for their dexterity on ships where they were kept as pets to kill rodents.

Other than their extra toes, the polydactyl cats look like ordinary house cats. They come in normal cat colors, solids, black and white, tabbies, and calicos. Their coats can be long or short haired. Hemingway was given his first cat by a sea captain. The cat, Snowball, produced more polydactyl cats and the feline family grew. Today there are between forty and fifty cats living on the property. A small cat cemetery is situated in the back of the property for those cats who have passed on. Hemingway's love for his cats has spawned a new name for the polydactyl cat, the Hemingway Cat.

In 1939, Hemingway left Pauline and the cats moving to Cuba with his new wife, Martha. He continued to visit Key West throughout the remainder of his life although his marriage to Martha lasted only four years. He married another female journalist, Mary Welsh. The couple lived in Cuba then retired in Idaho.

In his later years, Hemingway suffered from depression and paranoia in addition to high blood pressure and liver disease. During his final months, his wife, Mary, became distressed when he talked of destroying himself. She admitted him to a mental hospital where he received eleven electroshock treatments. Some believe that these treatments caused even more mental trauma in him diminishing some of his memories. After his release he made numerous suicide attempts, twice with a gun, once trying to jump from a plane then attempting to walk into the plane's propeller. He was committed a second time for more treatments.

Several days after his release from the hospital, on July 2, 1961, Ernest Hemingway went to his basement where he kept his gun collection. He shot himself with his favorite shotgun. His behavior in his final days was similar to that of his father prior to his suicide in 1928. Upon learning of his father's suicide, he remarked to his first wife that he'd probably "go the same way."

It was later determined that both Ernest and his father suffered from a congenital metabolic disease, hemochromatosis, an inability to metabolize iron which results in both mental and physical deterioration. Hemingway's sister, Ursula, and a brother, Leicester, also committed suicide. As would his granddaughter, Margaux, years later.

Shortly after his death, reports of his ghost in Key West cropped up. The sounds of his typewriter were often heard coming from his pool house studio. Visitors often see him on his balconies or on the porch of the house waving to them. Others have seen him walking the gardens with the cats. When Hemingway purchased the home, he claimed there were already resident ghosts. He reported seeing an old black woman and a well-dressed man from time to time. Shortly after he bought the property, human remains were found buried in the yard but authorities deemed them to be very old and probably from Native American times in an earlier Key West. He even kept one of the skulls that were dug up, on his desk.

Hemingway used to enjoy fishing off the banks of the Southernmost Point. Many people see the apparition of man, just standing there, staring into the sea. By the time they realize who he is, he vanishes or just walks away silently. Although he didn't die in Key West, the best years of life were spent there. And it is there that he has chosen to spend his afterlife.

Haunted La Concha Hotel

"There is no refuge from memory and remorse in this world. The spirits of our foolish deeds haunt us, with or without repentance." ~ Gilbert Parker

The ghost of Ernest Hemingway is not the only spirit to haunt the La Concha Hotel on Duval Street in the heart of Old Town. Built in 1924, the seven story hotel is the tallest in Key West. The hotel was been a favorite with writers, celebrities, gangsters, and politicians. Al Capone and his cronies frequented the hotel during "fishing trips" to Key West. Pulitzer Prize winning author, Tennessee Williams completed his play, *A Streetcar Named Desire*, at the La Concha.

Sometime in the late 1980s a dishonest attorney who was accused of embezzlement and under investigation decided to end his life at the La Concha. He checked into hotel and went up to the roof. There he used a tape recorder that he hoped would clear his name in the crime he had committed and make his own suicide look like a murder so his family could collect his insurance money.

He paced back and forth on the roof talking madly into his recorder. He accused his secretary with the crime and talked of people trying to kill him. He then made it sound as if he wasn't alone. He repeatedly begged into the recorder for his unknown assailant to not kill him. He screamed, "NO!"

The recorder was still on record, in his hand as his lifeless body lay on the ground below. The entire conversation along with the sounds of his screams as he fell recorded on the tape. But his efforts failed him. Authorities had already cleared the secretary and they had all the evidence they needed to pin the crime on him. Because of the way he fell it was also obvious that he threw himself over the railing of the rooftop rather than at the hands of a murderer. Because he committed suicide, his insurance policy refused to pay his family.

Suicide victims quite often return to haunt. Some believe they return because of religious beliefs, as many paths teach that suicide is the unforgivable sin. Some victims, fearing retribution, refuse to move on. In some cases, the victim has a change of heart when it's too late. One can only imagine what goes through the mind of someone who jumps from a building. In those final seconds, as one's life flashes before one's eyes, is there regret? No one knows. What we do know is that many suicides remain attached to the earth plane.

Guests at the La Concha have seen a man pacing on the roof back and forth talking to himself. Others have seen a man falling from the roof. Maybe the guilt he feels for the crime he committed, for the way he abandoned his family, leaving them confused and broke, causes this man to relive his crazed final moments in his own personal hell.

Another resident ghost of the hotel is a young waiter who worked there in the early 1980s. On New Year's Eve, 1983, he was doing a final cleanup of the fifth floor. His cart loaded with dishes, glasses, cups, and a trash bag full of confetti from the evening's celebration. It was about 1:45 AM January 1, as he bustled along with the heavy cart to the elevator in an attempt to finish for the evening. He backed up to the elevator doors and turned momentarily to hit the elevator down key. He heard the doors open indicating that the elevator had arrived. He backed up pulling the heavy cart through the doors, but before he realized what lie ahead, he dropped down into the elevator shaft, heavy cart and dishes following him. Due to some freak malfunction the elevator had stopped on the sixth floor directly above him, the doors opening on the fifth floor to an open shaft. He died on impact hitting the bottom floor of the shaft the cart on top of him. An hour passed before a guest complained that the elevator wasn't working. A maintenance employee shined a flashlight down the shaft and saw the man's body lying below.

This young man's death sets the perfect stage for a haunting. With a few exceptions, most hauntings are caused by violent, tragic, and untimely death compounded by very strong emotions. In his final minutes, he rushed his work, anticipating celebrating the New Year with friends and family. He was looking forward to enjoying what was left of the evening. His life was unexpectedly cut short, and violently. The shock and trauma on his final seconds of life would have left a serious energetic impression in the property.

Guests often feel a presence watching them on the fifth floor. Sometimes a cold breeze is felt whisking by. Housekeeping staff sometimes refuse to go to the fifth floor in fear of encountering the ghost. Wait staff find missing carts from the closet only to later find one sitting in front of an elevator. Some people hear the sounds of eighties music late at night on the fifth floor. Guests have happened upon a waiter pushing a cart slowly down the hallway, disappearing at the elevator. The poor soul relives his last few minutes of life again and again, perhaps looking for a way out, only to find that he never makes it out of the La Concha Hotel.

Ghosts of the Gulf

"Each life makes its own imitation of immortality." ~ Stephen King

Situated in the Gulf of Mexico directly off of Key West is Fort Zachary Taylor. Construction began in 1845 and continued into the 1850s. Work was slowed due to yellow fever outbreaks, hurricanes, and its remote location, surrounded completely by water with only a plank connecting it to the island. The fort fell into Union hands early on in the Civil War. The Union used it as an outpost to secure a location in the Gulf of Mexico. Parts of the structure were used as a hospital for yellow fever victims, others as a prison. Many an execution took place on its grounds.

During the Civil War, the U.S. Navy used the property as their Gulf Coast Blockade headquarters. Because it was able to deter many supply ships from entering and leaving Confederate ports along the gulf, the fort is believed to have been instrumental in the war ending as soon as it did. It was used again during the Spanish-American War in 1898,then again in both World Wars. Its last official use was during the Cuban Missile Crisis before becoming a National Historic Landmark.

During the yellow fever epidemics, an average of fifteen people a day died there and they were buried on the parade ground. Over the years, many thousands died in the fort.

Ghostly soldiers appear lining up in formation and gun shots are heard in the early morning hours. Every day at noon, screams and cries for mercy can be heard coming from what was the jail. The sound of the trap door snapping open from where the gallows hanged many criminals can be heard echoing through the empty bastions. The apparition of a young girl covered in burns is often seen in the former hospital area.

In 1968, excavations took place uncovering the largest collection of Civil War relics found anywhere. Volunteer Howard England, a Key West resident and civilian architect for the Navy, is responsible for not only recovering the artifacts but for his contributions in restoring and preserving the fort. The restoration took ten years. It is believed that England found the antiquities with the help of the ghost of Wendell Gardner, a Civil War soldier who had been stationed at the fort. Gardner's ghost directed England to the exact places to excavate. Gardner's family later confirmed that he had died of yellow fever many years before. It is believed that today the ghosts of Howard England and Wendell Gardner still haunt the fort.

Halfway between Key West and Cuba lie several tiny islands called the Dry Tortugas. Ponce de Leon named them "dry" because there was no fresh water and "tortugas" because of the abundance of turtles around the islands. Another abandoned fortress sits silently on the main island of Garden Key, Fort

Jefferson. Ironically, it is the largest masonry fortress in the Western Hemisphere although it was never utilized as a fort.

Called the "Gibraltar of the Gulf," construction on Fort Jefferson began in 1846. It took thirty years and forty million bricks to complete using mostly slave labor. Working conditions were harsh; storms along with deadly heat, mosquitoes, dysentery, scurvy, and typhoid killed many. The massive fortress was sixty feet tall, four hundred fifty feet long on each side, and five feet thick. A seventy foot wide moat eventually filled with man-eating sharks separated it from a sea wall. By the time it was complete, it had become obsolete as a fort so the government commissioned it as a federal prison, giving way to a new nickname, the "American Devil's Island," after a notorious French penal colony.

The prison was home to some one thousand prisoners and another five hundred prison employees and their families.

Most prisoners were Army privates convicted of desertion. Of the civilian prisoners, the most famous was Dr. Samuel Alexander Mudd, convicted of conspiracy in the assassination of President Abraham Lincoln.

On April 14, 1865, John Wilkes Booth shot President Lincoln at Ford's Theater and fractured his leg leaping from the balcony to the stage. Later in the early morning hours of April 15, he visited Dr. Mudd who splinted and bandaged his leg. Mudd was implicated along with others in the conspiracy but escaped the death penalty by one vote. He was given life in prison at Fort Jefferson. While working as a prison nurse in the infirmary, he attempted an escape and was moved to the guardhouse which Mudd referred to as "the dungeon." He was shackled at the ankles when allowed to work around the prison. Because of the attempted escape he was no longer allowed to work in the infirmary but as a carpenter. In Mudd's memoirs he described his treatment while in the dungeon as "brutal and degrading."

In August 1865, a yellow fever epidemic spread rapidly throughout the prison. The vast majority of inmates as well as the prison doctor succumbed to the deadly disease. Dr. Mudd was asked to step in to replace him. It took months but eventually Dr. Mudd managed to get the epidemic under control. Dr. Mudd was pardoned in 1869. Frail and sick he returned home to Maryland. Despite being cleared in any conspiracy in the President's assassination, Dr. Mudd never cleared his name as far as the general public was concerned. The expression "his name is Mud" actually stemmed from this. Dr. Mudd died in 1885 at only forty-nine years of age.

The fort remained a prison until the 1870s and was then abandoned. Today the empty fortress sits on the tiny desolate island with nothing more than the memories of the ghosts that howl in the night inside.

Geiger's Ghosts

"He like a rock in the sea unshaken stands his ground." ~ Virgil

The Audubon House and Gardens is the home of several entities. The house is named in honor of John James Audubon. But Audubon never stayed in the house. In fact, due to his intense fear of yellow fever, he never spent the night on the island. When he did his work in Key West, he preferred to sleep on his boat.

He visited the home in 1832. It is believed that many of his paintings were completed there. He cataloged eighteen different birds for his "Birds Of America" project. It was also there that Audubon first discovered the great blue heron. His portrait of the white crown pigeon includes an unusual cordia tree found in the front of the property. Audubon renamed the tree "Geiger Tree" in honor of Captain Geiger. A little known fact is that in order for Audubon to properly paint his masterpieces, he killed and stuffed the birds then posed them for his works of art. Today, the house showcases twenty-eight of his original pieces.

Numerous visitors and staff members claim to see what is believed to be Audubon's ghost wandering the lush one acre orchid filled garden that surrounds the house.

The house is the former home of Captain John Geiger, the island's first harbor pilot. Geiger made his fortune as a wrecker, retrieving salvage from sunken ships. He lived in the home with his wife, Lucretia, and their nine children. There is some speculation that Captain Geiger was also a pirate. It is believed that some of his fortune is still buried on the property.

Certain misfortunes cannot be avoided even by the very wealthy. Most of his children died from disease on the property. During the 1800s, threats of yellow fever and dengue fever were rampant in mosquito infested tropical climates. Dengue fever was also referred to as "bone crusher fever," due to its accompanying joint and muscle pain. Both diseases caused very high fever and were often fatal. The stone walkway in the back of property runs right through what was once the childrens' gravesites.

One of the rooms in the house was designated as the quarantine room in an attempt to separate the sick children and spare the healthy. It is also the room where one of Geiger's sons died after falling from a tree. The room is now a shrine to the children still filled with toys and roped off to the public. The ghosts of children do childish things. Employees tell of the chandelier that constantly has its light bulbs mysteriously unscrewed. Another employee has heard his name called out by the children.

When Captain Geiger died, his grandson who was also a wrecker, Captain Willy Smith inherited the property. Willy became a rather eccentric recluse. It is said that he eventually refused to leave his second story room. He lived there with no electricity or water and used a basket that he would lower to have provisions sent up to him. He didn't always use the outhouse in the back of the property causing an awful smell of urine in the room where he lived and eventually died.

The ghost of Captain Geiger and his wife, Lucretia, are also still wandering the property. A woman in a flowing blue dress has been seen in various parts of the house. She walks through a room then disappears as quickly as she appeared. Captain Geiger is usually seen as a shadowy figure standing on the balcony looking out to sea. He's said to also wander the grounds protecting his buried treasure. In the room that once belonged to Willy sometimes the smell of urine fades in and out.

The creepiest aspect of the house is the large oilograms that hang on its walls. During the nineteenth century bereaved families often had postmortem portraits made of their deceased loved ones, especially children. One such painting of a ten-year-old girl named Hannah depicted the child with a forlorn look on her face and vacant, staring eyes. Visitors were disturbed by its appearance so the staff moved Hannah to the children's room in a vacant corner where she cannot be seen by the public. Since such time, the sounds of children playing and laughing are heard coming from the room.

One spirit who used to wreak havoc in the home disappeared in 1997; no one knows why or how she left. But she is feared all throughout Key West because it is believed that she lives inside the body of an antiquated doll and that the doll wanders the island. Many believe it's no ordinary ghost living in that doll but the spirit of a demon.

The 1922 Bye-Lo doll originally belonged to Geiger's granddaughter and is valued at $1000.00. "Mrs. Peck" was donated to the house in the 1980s. The doll had been made in England, fashioned after a dead baby to look authentic. Her body was made of cloth and her head of wax, her coloring was corpse-like, pale with dark circles under her eyes. Her yellowish teeth made her look sickly. She was put in a white basket-like stroller in the corner of the children's room. Strange things manifested once the doll came to the house. Heat sensor burglar alarms began to go off nightly. Passers-by often reported seeing shadowy figures dancing to candlelight in the third floor room.

Mrs. Peck despised having her photo taken. In fact, she usually made sure that something would prevent her image from appearing in photographs. One television cameraman joked about the doll being haunted and when he set his camera down its door opened spilling out the film. Another photo was taken by an insurance company who was documenting the items in the house. The one photo taken of Mrs. Peck had a black bar going right over the doll. During the filming of a documentary, a television set blew up on site.

On January 6, 1997, the house management changed alarm companies. On that day the alarm in the children's room was off between 1:30 PM and 5:00 PM. When the staff returned the following day,

Mrs. Peck was gone. Since her departure, alarms no longer go off in the children's room.

Numerous newspapers and even tabloids announced the disappearance of what the *World Weekly News* dubbed "the demon doll." Despite mass media attention the doll was never recovered. All agree that if she was stolen, whoever took her would probably suffer terrible woes. There are some who believe that the doll was indeed possessed by some sort of spirit and that she simply left. Perhaps each time the alarm had gone off in the past, she may have been attempting her escape.

Still there remains the legend of a small withered figure, with yellow protruding teeth who roams the darkened streets of Old Town. Some say it's a demon in search of living souls disguised as an innocent child's toy. She's out there somewhere, waiting, and watching.

Dolly Dearest

"To see a doll of yourself is very weird and very neat at the same time." ~ Thuy Trang

Mrs. Peck is not the only haunted doll on the island. Another doll believed by some to be possessed is a cloth doll named Robert who sits in a glass encasement in the East Martello Museum.

In the late 1890s in Key West, there lived a well to do couple named Thomas and Minnie Otto. They had three beautiful children and a lavish home. They had many servants to cater to their every whim including a Jamaican nanny. In October, 1900, the Ottos welcomed a fourth child, a son, whom they named Robert Eugene.

The nanny had recently lost her own infant son the previous year to yellow fever. She immediately took to Gene, as he was called, as if he was her own. The newborn seemed to console her grief. Her growing affection for the baby spawned jealousy in Mrs. Otto.

Her husband however assured her that her adoration was completely normal given the loss of her own child. Still the mother felt uneasy. The more neurotic she became over the nanny's affections for her son, the more her husband defended the woman. This only served to cause more suspicion and anguish in Mrs. Otto. Despite her attempts to limit bonding of the two, Gene continued to become more attached to his nanny, and she to him.

Shortly before Gene's fourth birthday, the nanny began making his birthday gift. She spent countless hours sewing together a life-like doll made in the young boy's image. The doll was made of wire and cloth and stuffed with straw. Buttons were his eyes. For his crown, real hair saved from Gene's haircuts.

Some suspect there might have been some element of black magic involved when the doll was constructed. The superstitious believe that perhaps in her loss, she might have somehow used magic to store the soul of her own child in a crystal then inserted it into the doll as it seemed to have a life of its own.

It was customary at that time to give a child a doll bearing his or her likeness, so the family didn't question the gift. Gene was immediately enamored with the doll, calling it Robert after himself. The boy and his doll became inseparable. No sooner did the child receive the doll than strange things started occurring in the Otto home. Silverware would get thrown about in the dining room. Servants were locked out of rooms, clothing and bedding torn apart and left crumpled on the floor. Other beloved toys of Gene would be found mangled and mutilated. If blamed for anything wrong, Gene would always blame the doll. "Robert did it," he would insist.

Soon thereafter, for unknown reasons, Mrs. Otto insisted upon the dismissal of Gene's nanny. There are only mere speculations as to what really happened to cause her departure. Some suspect that maybe she had been a mistress of Mr. Otto and perhaps the child she had lost was his. Others contend that Mrs. Otto discovered that the woman was practicing black magic on the property. The latter seemed the least likely. Long after slavery was abolished, Southern men continued to keep servant women as mistresses. Gene was so distraught; even his mother didn't have the heart to remove the doll to which he had become so attached. Gene's behavior became increasingly odd as did his relationship with the doll. He would not eat at the family table unless a place was set for Robert. He slept with the doll. He took the doll everywhere he went. He even dressed like the doll.

Servants heard conversations between the boy and the doll swearing it was in two distinctly different voices. Late at night as Gene slept, the sounds of a child's footsteps and laughter could be heard throughout the house. The servants began to believe that the doll was cursed. Mrs. Otto began to believe the rumors herself after finding her son one day cowering in corner of his room and Robert seated on a chair above him, staring down at him. A great aunt convinced Mrs. Otto to lock Robert away in a sea chest in the attic. That evening, the old woman died, apparently from a stroke. Robert was given back to Gene.

Gene remained close to Robert until he left for Paris to pursue his art career. Robert was locked away in the family home, alone and ignored. It was there that he met his future wife, Anne. After Anne and Gene were married, they returned to the family house where they continued to reside. Gene resumed his peculiar relationship with Robert. He insisted on taking Robert everywhere the couple went. Robert sat at the dinner table when they ate. He even had a small bed for Robert in their bedroom. Anne hated Robert.

As Gene grew older, he built a room in the attic for Robert. He filled it with doll sized furniture and toys just for Robert. Eventually, Gene informed Anne that Robert was angry and demanded a room with a window. So Robert was moved to the turret room of the Victorian Mansion. Gene had been an ill-tempered child and became an even nastier adult. He grew abusive to Anne.

When angry, it's said he would lock her in a closet that was directly below Robert's room. Gene continued into his adult life blaming Robert for any misfortune he encountered.

Neighborhood children claimed to see Robert staring out of the window of the turret room. Some say he would move from window to window watching them. A contractor performing repairs on the home described an eerie encounter with Robert. He was making repairs in the room where Robert was seated in a chair. He kept feeling as if the doll was watching him.

From time to time, he would leave the room to retrieve tools. Upon returning each time, it had appeared as if the doll had moved but because he was busy, he didn't pay much attention. Upon completion of the repair he began to bring his tools back down the stairs. Suddenly, he heard a child's laughter behind him. He raced back into the room to find that Robert had not only changed positions, but was seated across the room. He checked the room looking for a child but found nothing.

As Gene aged, he became more eccentric and reclusive spending most of his time in the Turret Room with Robert. Gene died in that room with Robert at his side. After Gene's death, Anne rented out the home and planned her return to her family in Boston. She locked Robert in the attic room, and insisted that the rental agreement include a provision that no one was to unlock the room where Robert was kept. Tenants heard footsteps and a child's laughter coming from the locked room along with strange knocking sounds. Locked doors would open on their own and unlocked ones not open at all. Books would fly off of shelves across the room.

After her death, the house was sold and access to the locked room gained. The new owners had a ten-year-old daughter who eventually happened upon Robert and added him to her toy collection in her bedroom. No sooner was Robert brought into the child's room did she began waking in the middle of the night screaming, claiming the doll was attacking her.

To this day, she remains convinced that the doll was evil and trying to kill her. The girl's parents once again locked Robert in the attic, this time in a chest. Eventually, the house changed hands again and Robert was released. He was donated to the East Martello Museum. But the stories of Robert continue. Not only is Robert a haunted object, but it seems that whatever possesses Robert is able to leave the doll and haunt the Gene's former home, now the Artist House B&B.

People still report seeing the doll peering out of the windows of the turret room. Guests report the sounds of a small child laughing and running upstairs. Windows and doors open on their own.

In the museum, visitors claim that his expressions change. They are warned to pay proper respect to Robert as those who do not, are haunted by him. The museum has been flooded with letters from people begging Robert to remove his curse. One visitor reported that after visiting Robert, something followed her home. She claimed to see the silhouette of the doll outside her bedroom window. During which time, the electricity was out in her bedroom yet the rest of the house remained lighted. There are claims that Robert drains the energy of the living. Camera batteries die in his presence. Robert is said to have even caused several pace makers to stop working in his presence. According to museum employees, some visitors hear a tapping on the glass enclosure and turn to see his hand against the glass. Museum employees urge visitors to always ask permission from Robert before photographing him.

According to one museum employee, one man didn't and when he returned home, he died. Robert's encasement is surrounded by everything from love letters to birthday cards, along with letters asking him to remove their bad luck. The bad luck noted in the letters ranged from flat tires, stolen cameras, to hospital visits. When I visited the museum, the woman sitting at the front desk saw my camera and asked did I plan to photograph Robert. I told her that my visit was specifically to see him. She warned me not to take his photograph without asking his permission.

The museum itself is fairly creepy even without Robert's presence. Originally a fort built in 1862, though never used in battle, there seems to be a strong energy emitting from the building that can be felt upon arrival at the entrance. It was in 1862 that the largest yellow fever epidemic hit Key West taking many lives which could account for the eerie feeling in the area. Even walking the grounds, there is feeling of heaviness on the property.

During my visit, Robert seemed to change expressions. He appeared rather solemn at first glance but then seemed to be smiling. In some photos I've seen, he appears to be smiling, then as if he is scowling. Sometimes he even looks sad. Maybe it's just the angle, maybe it's the power of suggestion, or maybe, just maybe, something lives inside that little cloth and straw body. Even if he was just a figment of Gene Otto's imagination during his life, Gene himself might even have chosen to inhabit Robert in order to remain close to him. My respects go to Robert, nonetheless, just in case.

Strange Love

"Love can sometimes be magic. But magic can sometimes... just be an illusion." ~ Javan

Although there is no ghost associated with this story, the story itself is haunting. The ghastly saga began in 1899 in a dreary castle in Weimar, Germany, where Carl Tanzler grew up. His mother told him stories of ghostly woman in white who haunted the castle, believing it to be that of an ancestor who had died in 1765.

As a young boy, Carl's interests were that of physics, chemistry, flying machines, and astronomy, not of ghost tales. In college, he had no interest in dating at all. He created a laboratory in his home where he experimented with electricity and all matters of science. By the time he was twenty-four-years-old, he had obtained master's degrees in medicine, physics, mathematics, and philosophy.

Late one evening, as he studied in his laboratory, he claimed to have witnessed a strange event. He watched as a pencil levitated into the air then fell to the floor. A matchbox then lifted itself from the table and flew across the room. Before long, his papers and books were flung about by some unseen force. His table rose up to the ceiling causing the oil lantern to catch fire to the room. When he retreated to some draperies, however, there was no smoke, no ashes, and no heat. Then he heard a loud sound that likened to a gunshot. The glass disks on an expensive machine he had built had cracked all four of them right down the middle.

Believing that there was a prowler or prankster in the room, Carl retrieved a pistol from his desk drawer and walked about in search of the perpetrator. Much to his surprise, he was alone in the room. He describes chairs continuing to move about on their own, dancing about, as if mocking him.

The following morning he described the events to his mother who confirmed that the green room he used as his office and laboratory had been reputed as haunted for many years. That night he was awakened by the apparitions of two women. One was older with white hair and the other young and beautiful, with long, black hair. The older woman, whom he believed to be the ghost of his ancestor, the Countess Anna Constantia von Cosel spoke to him. She told him that he was destined to marry this young girl. The apparitions then quickly disappeared and the young Carl returned to his slumber. But this was a dream he would never forget.

Many years later, as he traveled through Genoa, he happened upon a gravesite whereupon stood a statue of a beautiful young girl who resembled the girl from his vision. He learned that her name was Elena and she had died at age twenty-two. He then claimed to see the apparition of the girl emerge from the statue and appear before him. She smiled and greeted him then disappeared. It was at this point that Carl became obsessed with "Elena" and vowed to find her again.

Carl traveled for many years eventually settling in Australia and working for the government as an electrical engineer and X-ray technician, all the while visits from the spirits continued. He received a strange visit from a spirit while living in Australia. He was awakened by footsteps and a key being inserted into his door lock. He saw a shadow of woman moving on the wall. He sat up under mosquito netting, both nightlights were blown out. He noted how impossible that was given that each light was in a different room and each was glass covered. He reached for his revolver and cocked it then he sat up in bed until dawn. He walked through the house and found nothing.

On March 7, 1912 Carl sat at dinner in the early evening as a storm raged outside. The house was peaceful as he enjoyed tea and a meal. At 7:00 pm the storm ceased and a figure of a woman covered in a white veil appeared in the doorway of his dining room. Her long black hair shown through her transparent veil and her dark eyes fixed on him. What became immediately apparent to him was that the woman was opaque. He remained calm, rose from his chair and asked, "What can I do for you, my lady?"

She didn't answer but she smiled and stretched out both hands, like a child. His hair raised and he was covered in cold shivers as he carefully walked towards her. As he touched her, he felt happy and elated; no longer apprehensive. He embraced her and felt as if he was floating in air. Then her body dissolved in his arms. His arms fell limp and fear gripped his heart as he had lost her again. Struck with horror that he had destroyed her with his arms, he began to panic. He stepped into the hall and she was there again, but this time at his side.

Carl described in his memoirs, "As I moved, she moved with me. Her feet did not touch the ground neither did mine. She smiled at me. She seemed to be at peace. It was as if I addressed an angel who was forbidden to speak, but understood all I said. I offered her to share my food and a cup of tea. I asked her permission to clear the table. I made a gesture as if I was going to retire to my bedroom. She stood immobile all night like a guardian angel."

In the morning the ghost followed him to his studio. For the following week, she watched him from the entrance of the hall. She followed him around the house. She stood near his bed all night like a guardian. She smiled but never spoke. He described "an incorporeal love between us which approached the divine." On the 7th day, she left. He believed that she was his intended bride. And he knew that one day they would be reunited.

Carl then fell into a deep depression. He fell ill and spent the next three months in a hospital with both typhoid and malaria fever. During his hospital stay he learned that his father had fallen into a coma on the exact day that he first saw the veiled apparition. His father died on the day the vision disappeared.

After his hospital stay, Carl spent four years in a British concentration camp due to his German citizenship. He built a pipe organ while in prison which he took with him to his native Germany once released. Eventually Carl married and had two daughters. It is unclear exactly when this took place as he oddly excluded any information about his wife and daughters in his memoirs. Messages from spirit led him to relocate in South Florida. His mind had been reinforced with the notion that he would find his Elena there.

Convinced he would find his love, at the age of fifty, Carl moved his family to Zephyrhills, Florida, in 1926, where he promptly abandoned them and set out for Key West. He changed his name to Count Carl von Cosel and secured a job as a radiology technician in the tuberculosis ward of a local hospital. Like Ed Leedskalnin, Carl was a tinkerer. He built an airship, played with strange electronic devices, and built a homemade organ as he waited for his love to cross his path. No one will ever know for sure if Carl von Cosel truly was given divine messages that were possibly misinterpreted or if he was simply a schizophrenic with a distorted internal dialogue that led him on his quest.

Maria Elena Milagro de Hoyos was only twenty-two-years-old when her family admitted her to the facility for tuberculosis in 1930. On April 22, Carl was asked to take a blood test of the girl. He hardly looked at her as he entered the room. He did notice that her ears were too beautiful to maul so he took her hand to draw her blood. He noted that her hands were unusually small. He described in his memoirs first seeing Elena, "As the needle struck, the hand twitched a little and it was from there that I lifted my head for the first time to say, 'I'm very sorry to have caused you pain, forgive me please.' Her face had been hidden by her hand so that I had hardly seen it when I entered the room but now she withdrew he hand to answer me and I looked into a face of unearthly beauty. The face of my dreams and visions; the face of a bride which had been promised to me by my ancestor 40 years before. I was so thunderstruck, I hardly heard her say, 'It didn't hurt much, please excuse my nervousness.'"

Carl felt at this point that he had finally found, literally, the girl of his dreams. Upon learning that she had tuberculosis, he became obsessed with curing her. Uninterested in the old man, she rebuked his affections. Nonetheless, in an attempt to secure an emotional attachment, he became obsessed with treating the dying young woman.

Elena's family, very poor and grasping at straws to help their daughter, invited von Cosel to their home to try unconventional methods to cure her. He made elixirs of various herbs including some that contained specks of gold. He incorporated radiation therapy along with electric shock treatments in a futile attempt to cure the girl. During one of his home visits, he notices that she has a photograph of St. Cecelia above her bed. This he takes as further confirmation that divine intervention had led him to Elena.

In addition to medical experiments in an attempt to save her, Carl showered her with gifts hoping to "cheer her up." He wrote letters to her offering medical advice mixed with his constant confirmations of his undying love for her.

During her treatments, he proposed marriage to her several times. He even presented an engagement ring to her hidden in a bouquet of roses. He bought her watches, clothing, anything she wanted. But his love was unrequited. Elena was always polite to him but made it very clear that she had no romantic interest. The relationship existed only his mind. Everything that he did was based on fabrications he created in his mind, having nothing to do with reality.

Eventually his aggressive advances scared the girl and her family causing them to refuse further medical treatments. But Carl was not a man who could accept rejection. The more Elena pushed him away, the more aggressively he pursued her. He visited her daily begging her to continue treatments. Elena had started feeling better and felt she didn't need his help any longer. Although he had a true interest in curing her, his motives were based more on his need to possess her rather than sincere interest in her well-being. His was a selfish, obsessive love.

In an effort to keep Carl away from Elena the family literally packed up and changed residences overnight. For weeks, Carl wandered the streets of Key West in search of the new residence until he found her again. He informed the family that he was "in charge now for good." It appears that Carl literally stalked and terrorized this girl and her family. Any attempt on her part to discourage him was interpreted by him as her merely being modest. Any attempt on the family to keep him away, he interpreted as interference. In his mind, he shared a relationship with her. To her and her family, it was a hostage situation.

It was only after Elena's death that her family agreed to accept help from Carl. The poor family had little means to pay for a funeral and burial for their daughter. Carl paid for a lavish funeral for Elena but was horrified when her family buried her beneath the ground. Unable to bear the thought of his beautiful beloved rotting in the ground he convinced the family to allow him to build a mausoleum for her. Elena was exhumed and moved to a new metal casket that Carl had outfitted with a formaldehyde-filled incubator to preserve her beauty forever. But even death could not pull Carl out of denial. He told himself, "She is not dead." Unbeknownst to her family, he kept a key to the mausoleum and visited her nightly, bringing her flowers and gifts.

He maintained his affair of the heart with the corpse for two years. He claimed to have been visited by her ghost on several occasions. He invented conversations with the deceased girl becoming convinced that she was begging him to free her from her prison. He heard Elena's voice singing a song to him. The song was a Spanish ballad about a lover who opens the grave of his dead bride, La Boda Negra, which means "The Black Wedding."

Each night, her sweet voice sang to him the haunting song, "En una horrenda noche, hizo pedazos; el mármol de la tumba; abandona da cavo; la tierra y se llevó en susbrazos; el rigidoesqueleto de suamada. (English: In a horrific night shattered; the abandoned marble tomb; He dug the ground and carried in her arms; the rigid skeleton of his beloved."

Elena's death threw Carl over the edge of sanity leaving the remainder of his life nothing more than a morbid fantasy.

Resurrection

"Death is the only pure, beautiful conclusion of a great passion." ~ David Herbert Lawrence

Late one night in April 1933, Carl dressed himself in his wedding finery making his way to the cemetery. Using a handmade cart that he designed specifically for his task, he stole Elena's casket and pushed it through town to his home. There he felt as if the entire cemetery came alive.
He wrote:
"A wonderful elated feeling took complete possession of my entire being, as though a second spirit has entered my soul. It seemed that a bodyguard of veiled angels had formed on both sides and were coming along with us and great inspiration filled me then. It made me feel like a victor, holding the triumphal entry in a world forgotten and buried. I felt secure, protected, and invulnerable. No matter what was coming against us now, nothing could harm either of us anymore.

There was no place for the living here on this blackest night. All of the cemetery was alive with souls which came out of the graves from all sides, it was indeed like a festival of the departed, as they moved up on all sides. It was like a great divine wedding march for me taking place. It could not be a funeral march, for all seemed happy and joyful and interested in silent admiration, watching as the white forms of angels filed past with me and Elena in their midst. They were everywhere, none blocking our way, but melting out of our way. It seemed as if they had never seen such a celebration in this cemetery before. It was as if all were delighted and desirous to help us..."

But as Carl attempted to lift the coffin and hoist it over the cemetery wall, the ground upon which he stood caved in. Carl fell into a shallow sink hole, Elena's coffin, and the cart falling on top of him crushing his felt wedding hat. With all of his determination and strength, he lifted the coffin off himself, finally managing to push atop the fence, then finally over to the other side. It was then that Carl noticed that a putrid smelling liquid was dripping on him from inside the coffin. The foul smelling ooze dripped down his neck and all over his black satin trimmed wedding jacket. He finally made his way to a small dismal shack that he had rented for Elena. Having no running water, he removed his clothing and washed himself with whiskey.

Much to his horror when he opened the casket he found that his incubator failed to preserve her. All he was left with was bones, rotted flesh, and an oozing green liquid. But true love conquers all.

Heartbroken, the old man set out to reconstruct his beloved Elena. He recorded in his memoirs:

"My very soul was tortured when I saw her awful condition. I resolved that I would help her out of this awful mess at once. She was my beloved bride. My promise to care for her was sacred.

With the greatest care, I now detached the uppermost layer of clothing, which were overgrown and eaten up with slimy molds. I then got a large bucket and deposited into it rags until it was filled. Careful, peeling off around her head, face, and chest first, I found many pieces had become glued to the skin. All of those which didn't come off easily, I left on her body to soak for the time being, as it might injure her delicate skin, which I wanted to keep intact. The bucket was heaping full and heavy. It had to be removed quickly as the odor was overpowering."

Carl dumped the bucket filled with putrid water and rags into the emerald gulf waters. He then meticulously began the process of creating his new Elena. He used piano wire to hold her fragile fingers together and cloth rags to simulate her muscles. He covered her with a skin of silk and wax. During her radiation treatments when she was ill, her hair had fallen out. Carl, of course, had saved it. He tediously inserted each hair into her newly made scalp. He used lotions and electric shock treatments to assist in preserving her. He made attempts to cover the stench of the rotting corpse with oils and perfumes.

He remarked of her condition:

"I could find little time to rest, to examine her body, and study its condition more thoroughly. I looked into the deep fallen cavities of her eyes, like deep empty black holes, I saw her dried up lips, slightly parted with her white teeth gleaming between them. And when looking so long and deep into those black openings, where once her beautiful eyes shone

so bright, it was strange indeed; it seemed as if a pair of pupils were forming again, deep inside, and were looking at me as from the bottom of a well, straight and serious.

By further examination, I was not surprised to find small maggots of the gnat larvae type which were feeding on blood around her head and ears and around the skin on her abdomen..."

As he rebuilt her, tending to her body as if it were merely injured but still alive, he spent countless hours conversing with her, and playing his organ and singing to her. Her once beautiful ebony eyes were now made of glass, staring blankly. Her facial features were re-sculpted using mortician's wax. The process took months to complete. Carl was convinced that at some point, Elena would come back to life. He infused her body with vitamins and herbal supplements. He remarked, *"...she improved daily, and even her living expression returned."*

As he made the finishing touches to his masterpiece, laying her out in a coffin, he told her, *"Darling, I love you more than ever before. If it were not so, I would not have taken you to me. Then kissing her dry lips, and breathing deeply into her lungs until her bosom rose, I unpacked her bridal gown and covered her body with it. I draped her with the silk veil and adorned her head and hair with a golden crown. She looked so wonderful now, I could not resist the wondrous spell and trembling with burning love, I sank gently into the coffin with her and kissed her as if she were alive."*

He moved her body to a bed that he had bought for her, surrounding her with flowers. He called her "the beautiful secret." For eight years, Carl lived his secret life with Elena. He "fed" her fluids with a feeding tube to keep her hydrated and nourished. He used electrical currents in attempts to reanimate his lifeless mummy. He believed that she was indeed coming back to life. He wrote, "Her hair, which had been flat and lifeless in her coffin, had become alive again, taking its own characteristics waves and curls. Her hair even regained its electrical properties; being attracted to my hands when they came near it. No matter what the cause, it indicated life, though different than before."

He even made and sold postcards of a photograph depicting a waxen bride laid out on a bed.

In 1940, Elena's sister became suspicious after not hearing from von Cosel or seeing him visiting the tomb in so many years so she called upon him for a visit. He welcomed her inside and immediately took her to the bedroom to visit. She was of course horrified to see the waxen, decomposing body of her sister lying on the bed in her bridal dress. Carl told her that he and Elena were happy. He thanked her for stopping by and told her to visit again soon. Horrified by the discovery, the sister contacted authorities who raided his home and found the corpse still intact.

The most shocking findings were made by the doctor who conducted the autopsy revealing that Carl had not only lived with a corpse for eight years but had been intimate with it. He later disclosed, "I made the examination in the funeral home. The breasts really felt real. In the vaginal area, I found a tube wide enough to permit sexual intercourse. At the bottom of the tube was cotton, and in an examination of the cotton, I found there was sperm. Then I knew we were dealing with a sexual pervert."

But Carl was not some sexual deviant who delighted in making love to a corpse because she was dead. He was a human being who was so obsessed, and in his own warped way, in love with a woman, he could not bear to let her go. A true necrophiliac would have gone on in pursuit of another dead body; von Cosel wanted only Elena, accepting her in whatever form he had to. The extent to which his delusions and obsession caused him to cross those boundaries makes for a very sad and tragic tale of unrequited love.

The definition of necrophilia, according to the DSM-IV-TR, is "the presence, over a period of at least six months, of recurrent and intense urges and sexually arousing fantasies involving corpses which are either acted upon or have been markedly distressing."

Stephen J. Hucker, Consulting Forensic Psychiatrist at University of Toronto, wrote in an article, "In all cases, there is undoubtedly sexual preference for a corpse rather than a living woman. When no other act of cruelty – cutting into pieces, etc., - is practiced on the corpse, it is probable that the lifeless condition itself forms the stimulus for the perverse individual. It is possible that the corpse – a human form absolutely without will – satisfies an abnormal desire, in that the object of desire is seen to be capable of absolute subjucation, without the possibility of resistance.

(http://www.forensicpsychiatry.ca/paraphilia/necro.htm)

Not only did von Cosel not prefer Elena to be dead, it does not appear that he even believed that she was dead.

During his trial, von Cosel confessed that he had built an airship to take Elena away to allow radiation from outer space heal her body and restore her life. Somehow the court declared von Cosel sane but was unable to prosecute him due to the statutes of limitations on grave robbing having expired. Necrophilia was not a crime in Florida at the time.

Oddly, Elena's body was shown publicly at the Dean-Lopez Funeral Home before being buried in a secret vault. More than six thousand onlookers paid their respects to the waxen corpse of Elena prior to her burial. A man later recalled the ghastly sight he had seen at only ten-years-old, "I've never been able to forget that sight. It didn't even look human anymore. So much reconstruction and decay…it was the scariest thing I'd ever seen. Her face was as odd whitish color that looked more like a wax dummy than a woman's face. And she had horrible black, starring glass eyes. I still dream about that sight."

In July, 1952, von Cosel was found dead in his home slumped over a life-sized replica of Elena that he allegedly created from a death mask he had previously made from her face. But was it a replica? An individual who was present at her burial claimed that the coffin was filled with bricks and that Elena's body was actually returned to von Cosel.

When he was released from prison, von Cosel wrote his memoirs giving his side of the story. He wrote:

"When in November, 1940, I was finally released from prison, I was a very bitter man. Charges had been brought against me that I was a violator of the grave, a ghoul, a fiend of society. There was an avalanche of misrepresentations, of sensational press stories which accused me of being a sexual pervert, a necromancer, a maniac, while being confined for court hearing. Worst of all they had removed Elena's body, that body which I had treated, first to preserve it in its unearthly beauty, and then to reunite with its soul which always was with me in the scientific efforts of over seven years. What made these misfortunes even heavier was the fact that, at the time of my release, I was sixty-four-years-old, and had lost my employment through Roosevelt's retrenchment, had lost my home on the beach of Florida, which had been destroyed by hoodlums before my captivity and with the war restrictions, found myself almost without means of existence.

With my whole life thus deranged, I lived for a time as a recluse amongst the rubble of my laboratory, using the air- plane, which I had built for Elena, as a shelter. But then a strange and unexpected turn of affairs brought me back to life. I discovered that there was human decency left in this world. From all parts of America and even from foreign countries hundreds of letters poured in and thousands of visitors came to see me, not from idle curiosity, but from humane sympathy. In their eyes I had not committed a crime. Gradually faith recovered and hope returned into my heart. I decided that it was my duty to answer comprehensively those thousands of questions I had been asked in connection with my life, and my love for Elena. I decided also that it was my duty to clear myself in the eyes of the public of the false accusations which bad been raised. In short, I found it necessary to tell my story, to remove this specter of ignorance.

So in the cabin of Elena's airship, where her coffin had rested for so long, I sat down and wrote this account. My position was cramped in the pilot seat and made all the more uncomfortable, because war regulations made it necessary to remove the wheels from the plane, so that my quarters were not only extremely narrow but slanting backward. I am no professional writer; I am not a poet; but I have a little gift of painting, and so I have tried to express in pictures what I could not say in words. In this manner, happiness of a kind came back to me; my life again has a purpose; although it is sad that these pictures (seen by visitors at my place) cannot be reproduced in this magazine.

Admittedly my experiments in resurrecting Elena were partly successful. Too often my work was interrupted and disturbed by outside circumstances beyond my control. But I am not giving up. I feel that the invaluable experience already gained lends itself as a reassurance that new experiments could be crowned with success. Elena's body, true enough, is now interred, but her dying wish that she and I should live together has been granted to both of us. She is with me as I write this, she advises me. It is her hand which, I feel, is leading my pen.

So then, I wish to thank, through this account, all those thousands of kind-hearted and big-hearted friends who have come to my support in my hour of need. It was their faith in me which has restored me to new life; it is to them I dedicate this book, and to my Elena, as she was the first who visited me while in jail."

Carl Tanzler von Cosel Key West, Florida, in the winter of 1940-41.

Carl's memoirs were published in 1947 in Amazing Adventures magazine. They were republished in 1988 then disappeared again.

To this day, no one other than a few at the Dean-Lopez Funeral Home know the location of Elena's gravesite. Many believe that because of the trauma she experienced in the final months of her life and for years after her death, that her spirit will never find peace. They believe that her spirit will eternally be wandering the narrow streets of Key West. And what of Carl's ghost?

Many believe that he too haunts the island. Still trying to spend eternity with his immortal beloved.

Final Thoughts

"We shall see that at which dogs howl in the dark, and that at which cats prick up their ears after midnight." ~ H.P. Lovecraft

The stories contained herein have been compiled over several years and numerous visits to Miami and the Keys. I first visited Miami in the late 1990s. I felt an intense urge to stay in one of the historic Art Deco hotels in South Beach. My days were spent sightseeing and eating in the fabulous restaurants throughout the city. At night I felt drawn to the ocean. I experienced an inexplicable feeling walking along the beach late at night with the neon lights shining through the palm trees that lined the walkways along the beach highway. It was as though I had been there before. Something about the beach felt comfortable and familiar. For the remainder of my stay, I immersed myself in the food, the music, and the glamour that is Miami Beach, always returning for late night walks along the surf. When I left Miami, I knew that I would return again. It did not occur to me at that time how connected I would eventually become to the city.

I returned in 2003. I had written a screenplay about the New Orleans underworld and could not resist including a Miami connection. I spent several days filming B roll for the film, "Silent Scream."

Schedules and budgets were tight so I left Miami feeling that I did not have enough time to relive the memories of my first visit. I vowed to return.

It was not until after Hurricane Katrina that I had the opportunity to get back to Miami for some serious research. By that time I had spent hours researching the area and become interested in several haunted locations near South Beach. Little did I know at the time that I would find much more than ghost stories and haunted buildings. While there I took sightseeing tours, pulled news articles, and interviewed locals. At night I would walk along the beach and feel that familiar sensation that had been beckoning me to return.

I experienced a completely different sensation when I made a late night visit to a local park in Coconut Grove. It was a magical feeling. Shadows darted around the large trees, and whispering voices echoed in the darkness. The park was alive with nature spirits. I could feel their energy as they scurried about like dancing fairies. A vibration from an underground spring could be felt beneath my feet. It was a much lighter feeling than I had felt in some of the sites where gruesome murders had been committed.

Every neighborhood has its own vibe. Whether it's the high intensity pulse of South Beach, the regal stillness of Coral Gables, the magical floating feeling of Coconut Grove, or the laid back easiness of Key West, each possesses a personality all its own that can be found nowhere else. As I traveled through one area of the city to another, I felt I was passing through an energy vortex each with its own distinct differences.

Once I began delving into the mysteries and murders I felt drawn in even more. One story was more intriguing than the next. Every time I visited I found something I had not found before; and a reason to return. Miami and the Keys are hotbeds for the weird and arcane.

Even if one isn't searching for the macabre, the area has many amenities that make it worth visiting. There is a rich, diverse culture that can be enjoyed regardless of one's tastes. Miami and the Keys continue to amaze and intrigue its visitors enticing them to return again and again.

Bibliography

http://www.bermudatriangle.org
www.forensicpsychiatry.ca/paraphilia/necro.htm

The Great One: The Life and Legend Of Jackie Gleason, William A. Henry, Doubleday, 1992

Ghosts Of The Air, Martin Caidin, Galde Press, Inc. November 1, 1994

Ghosts Of Flight 401, John G. Fuller, Berkley February 15, 1983

Miami Herald, article, "Edward Leedskalnin Rock Gate," 1945

Miami Herald, article, "Myths Over Miami," Lynda Edwards, June 5, 1997

Miami Herald, article, "Coral Castle," Phoebe Flowers, October 31, 2001

Fate Magazine, article, "Coral Castle," Frank Joseph, 1998

The Energy Grid, Bruce Cathe

The Enigma Of Coral Castle, Ray N. Stoner, Bradford Institute of Ultra Science, January 1, 1983

Bermuda-Triangle.Org "UFOs? Aliens? Area 51 Revealed," Ki Mae Heussner, April 10, 2009

Miami Herald, article "Myths Over Miami," Lynda Edwards Thursday, Jun 5 1997

"The Moon's Effect on Menstruation, Conception and General Health," Carole Carlton article, healthandgoodness.com

Expert Law Library article, "Serial Killers - A Homicide Detective's Take," By Lieutenant Nelson Andreu (Retired) Miami Police Department, Submitted May, 2005

Miami New Times News, "The Believers," Art Levine, Thursday, May 4,1995

Miami New Age Spirituality Examiner, "Alien Entities seen in Miami, Florida," Curtiss Massie, September 4, 2009

TruTv Crime Library, "A Million Dollar Murder," David Krajicek

Miami New Times News, "They Walk Among Us," Art Levine Thursday, May 4, 1994

TruTv Crime Library, "What Makes Serial Killers Tick?" Shirley Lynn Scott

TruTv Crime Library, "Murder in Miami – Joyce and Stan Cohen," David Krajicek

American Journal of Psychiatry, "The Threat to Kill," John Marshall Macdonald

"Necrophilia: An analysis of 122 cases involving necrophilic acts and fantasies. Bulletin of the American Academy of Psychiatry and the Law," Rosman, J. & Resnick, P. (1989)

Journal of New York Folklore, "Articles, Legends, &Quests," Libby Tucker, Volume 32

The Haunted places: The national directory: Ghostly abodes, sacred sites, UFO's, Dennis William Hauck, Penguin Publishing,2002

http://www.mayhem.net/Crime/conde.htmlTruT vCrime

Library, "Andrew Cunanan; After Me, Disaster,"

Joseph Geringer Saving South Beach, M. Barron Stofik, University Press of Florida, 2005

Miami, Then and Now, Carolyn Klepser and Arva Moore Parks, Thunder Bay Press, 2002

Death By Design, Lee Urness as told to Dave Racer, Airleaf Press, 2006

Miami New Times News, "The Suitcase Murders," Joanne Green, May 24, 2007

TruTV Crime Library, "A Killer's Rampage," Katherine Ramsland

TruTV Crime Library, "Dr. Steven Egger: Expert on Serial," Katherine Ramsland

Strange Key West, Matthew Sean Casey, Phantom Press, 2003

Haunted Key West, David L. Sloan, Phantom Press, 2003

Ghosts Of Key West, David L. Sloan, Phantom Press, 2003

Magnetic Current, Edward Leedskalnin, 1945

New York Times, article, "Locate The Valbanera, Sunk In Gulf Storm, But No Trace Of The 450 Passengers She Carried," September 20, 1919

Florida's Ghostly Legends and Haunted Folklore: South and Central Florida, Volume 1, Greg Jenkins, Pineapple Press, 2005

Key West Art & Historical Society University of Wisconsin School of Medicine, article, Psychopaths' Brains Show Differences in Structure and Function, 2011

Florida Times Union, article, "The Haunted Doll of Key West is gone," Bill Foley, January 22, 1997

Weekly World News, article, "Demon Doll Disappears," Mike Foster, February 25, 1997

Associated Press article, "Haunted Doll Vanishes From Key West Home," January 14, 1997

Sun Sentinel, article, "Dancing With The Devil Doll," Matt Schudel, October 26, 1997

TruTVCrime Library, "A Killer's Rampage," Katherine Ramsland

TruTV Crime Library, "Henry Lee Lucas," Katherine Ramsland

Programmed To Kill, David McGowan, iUniverse, Inc., 2004

Hand Of Death, Max Call, Vital Issues Press, 1985

"The Twisted Life of Serial Killer Ottis Elwood Toole," Fox News Archives

Huffington Post, article, "Ottis Toole: Adam Walsh's Killer," December 16, 2008

Eat Thy Neighbour: A History of Cannibalism, Daniel Diehl, Mark P. Donnelly, The History Press, 2009

Secrets Of Elena's Tomb, Carl von Cosel, 1947
Miami New Times News, article,

"Something From The X-Files They're calling the Asian snakehead 'the Frankenfish'" Carlos Harrison, August 22, 2002 http://www.anstaskforce.gov/spoc/swamp_eel.php

ABC News, "Hotel Heir Widow Charged in Husband's Death," Scott Mayerwitz, July 8, 2010

Miami Herald, article, "Ghost Hunters Say Deering Estates Ground Zero For Lost Spirits," 2010

Miami Herald, article, "Fontainebleau hotel heir's widow charged in mother-in-law's death," Diana Moskovitz, April 16, 2011

http://www.ghosttheory.com/2009/10/22/full-body-apparition-at-miami-estate, photo by Javier Ortega, October 22, 2009

Miami Herald, article, "Full Body Apparition at Miami Estate?" Howard Cohen

Chariots Of The Gods, Erich von Däniken, Berkley Trade, 1999

Florida's Past: People and Events That Shaped the State, Gene Burnett, Pineapple Press, 1997

Biogeography Seminar, Zoology Department, University of Illinois, "The Occurrence of Wild Apes in North America," Loren Coleman, 1973

The Apes, Vernon Reynolds, E.P. Dutton, 1967

Discover other fine publications at:

http://www.darkoakpress.com

www.ingramcontent.com/pod-product-compliance
Lightning Source LLC
LaVergne TN
LVHW011416080426
835512LV00005B/94